RAF
in Camera
1950s

RAF

in Camera

Keith Wilson

Pen & Sword
AVIATION

First published in Great Britain in 2015 by
Pen & Sword Aviation
an imprint of
Pen & Sword Books Ltd
47 Church Street
Barnsley
South Yorkshire
S70 2AS

ISBN 978 1 47382 795 0

A CIP catalogue record for this book is available from the British Library

Typeset in Helvetica by
Mac Style Ltd, Bridlington, East Yorkshire
Printed and bound in China by Imago

Pen & Sword Books Ltd incorporates the imprints of Pen & Sword
Archaeology, Atlas, Aviation, Battleground, Discovery, Family History,
History, Maritime, Military, Naval, Politics, Railways, Select, Transport,
True Crime, and Fiction, Frontline Books, Leo Cooper, Praetorian Press,
Seaforth Publishing and Wharncliffe.

For a complete list of Pen & Sword titles please contact
PEN & SWORD BOOKS LIMITED
47 Church Street, Barnsley, South Yorkshire, S70 2AS, England
E-mail: enquiries@pen-and-sword.co.uk
Website: www.pen-and-sword.co.uk

Contents

Foreword

The Air Historical Branch is the internal history office of the Royal Air Force and, amongst its many functions within that wider role, it maintains an archive of official photographs tracing the history of the Service. We are delighted to have the opportunity to publish this volume, which covers a particularly interesting decade in which the RAF not only found itself in the frontline of the Cold War but also involved in the many conflicts associated with the withdrawal from the empire.

The 1950s saw the transition from propeller to jet aircraft in full swing. Many of the venerable Second World War veterans – Lancasters, Mosquitoes and Sunderlands – were still soldiering on, often on the more distant stations, alongside the first-generation jets such as the Vampire. Meanwhile, a new generation of jets was entering service whose names still cause the hairs on many an enthusiast's neck to stand up: the immortal symmetry of the Hawker Hunter, vying with the more brutal lines of the English Electric Lightning and the delta-winged Gloster Javelin. Not least of the jet fighters' achievements was that they rekindled some of the excitement of the inter-war flying displays as the speed and noise of these new chariots gave full rein to the display teams' flamboyance. For an image of sheer power, however, little can compete with the V-bombers. Perhaps most impressive of all

the Avro Vulcan, and even more so when in the all-white paint scheme and carrying a Blue Steel, itself the harbinger of the missile age epitomised by the Thor intermediate-range ballistic missile (IRBM).

More prosaic, perhaps, but just as vital and as hard-working, were the transport aircraft: the improbable shape of the Blackburn Beverley contrasting with the elegance of the de Havilland Comet.

While the 1950s saw the rise of the jet, it also saw the dawn of the military helicopter. The Sycamores and Whirlwinds heralded a new era of the aircraft in a variety of roles, giving unparalleled flexibility and mobility to the British Army in many far-flung regions of the globe. It is therefore entirely fitting that the last photograph in the book depicts a Whirlwind of the Queen's Flight, thus giving the royal seal of approval and confirming that the helicopter really had 'arrived'.

The aircraft in this book have now departed the Service – with the ever-faithful Canberra the last to go – but the photographs of them in their heyday bear testimony to their sterling service and to the immense contribution they made to the defence of Britain's interests across the world.

SEBASTIAN COX BA MA FRSA
Head of the Air Historical Branch (RAF)

Acknowledgements

A project of this nature requires the help and support of many people, who have contributed in different ways to make the book possible. The author would like to offer his sincere thanks to the following:

Sebastian Cox at the Air Historical Branch, RAF Northolt, for providing the branch's support and access to the collection of images, along with his encouragement and sense of humour.

At Pen & Sword Books, I would like to thank Laura Hirst, Michelle Tilling and Matthew Blurton for their considerable input at key stages during the book's production and for keeping me on track whenever I wavered.

My very special thanks must go to Lee Barton at the Air Historical Branch for his unwavering enthusiasm, vision and attention to detail. Without your considerable help and support, this book would not have been completed. Thank you Lee!

Thanks are also due to the staff at the Imperial War Museum for their additional caption information.

Finally, sincere thanks to my wife Carol and sons Sam and Oliver. Thank you for your patience and support throughout the project. I couldn't have done it without you.

Introduction

Following the end of the Second World War, the immediate task of the Royal Air Force was to return to normal, peacetime conditions and the RAF was faced, for the second time in its history, with the problems of adjusting to peace after a major war. At the conclusion of the war, the total strength of UK service personnel totalled almost 5 million and the RAF contingent was estimated at around 1.3 million. Various statistics are available, each providing variations, but one RAF source document suggests that the total number of aircraft held on strength (including aircraft held in storage) amounted to 61,584.

Abroad, the RAF played its part (alongside the British Army, the Royal Navy and other Allied forces) in the vast clearing-up operation in Europe, the Middle East and the Far East.

At home, the RAF had to demobilise its huge forces as quickly and as smoothly as possible. The run-down of the RAF was more orderly and gradual than it had been in 1919 but, even so, discontent at poor conditions and the seemingly slow rate of repatriation led to a strike by airmen at RAF Seletar in Singapore and other disturbances at RAF Drigh Road, Karachi. By 1947, just less than a million men and women had been demobilised and the overall strength was down to less than 300,000. Aircraft held on strength had reduced drastically to 20,430.

Although Britain had ended the Second World War as one of the victorious Allies, the country was almost bankrupt after the vast outlay of national resources during the war. The first years of peace were blighted by rationing and austerity which exceeded those of the war years. Severe financial problems, coupled with the debilitating effect of nearly six years of war, made the task of redirecting the nation's war-making capacity to meet civilian peacetime needs very difficult.

By the end of the Second World War the jet, missile and nuclear age had arrived. The problems for the British Government and the RAF were whether Britain should develop its own atomic weapons and, if they were to be developed, what type of aircraft would be required to drop them. The Labour Government of Clement Attlee, which came to power in June 1945, decided that the United Nations was not strong enough to enforce any international control over atomic energy (and weapons) development. If the USA was not to have a monopoly of the new weapons, Britain had to develop its own nuclear weapons in order to safeguard its own security. After much political soul-searching and despite strong opposition by some members of the Labour Party, that decision was made on 8 January 1947.

Interestingly, the Air Staff had anticipated the decision by issuing a requirement for an atomic bomb in August of 1946. They had also issued – in November 1946 – a draft requirement for a new bomber that could deliver the atomic bomb. The specification was for a four-engined bomber with a greater range, twice the speed and twice the height over the target of any existing bomber.

On 9 January 1947, the day after the government's decision to develop an atomic bomb, the leading aircraft manufacturers were invited to design and build the new bomber. These two decisions, along with the doctrine of the strategic air bombardment, were the foundations of a strategic nuclear deterrent force – the V-force of Bomber Command – whose creation and deployment was the single most important and costly activity of the RAF between 1945 and 1969.

Bringing a strategic nuclear force into operation took nearly ten years after those decisions were made. During that time the Western deterrent was in the hands of the strategic air forces of the United States and the political leaders of the West were primarily occupied with the possibility that the Cold War could escalate into a third world war. The confrontational situation in Europe at the time of the Berlin Airlift had already been apparent. It led to USAF B-29 Superfortress bombers being deployed to the UK as well as the creation of the North Atlantic Treaty Organization (NATO) in 1949. Along with the outbreak of the Korean War in 1950, it also led to the largest ever peacetime UK defence budget to provide for an expansion of men and equipment: £4,700 million was to be spent over three fiscal years between 1951 and 1954, compared with less than £800 million spent annually before 1950. In addition, the recall of reservists and the extension of National Service to two years gave an active strength of nearly 900,000 for the three services; RAF strength was over 270,000, of which around one-third was National Servicemen.

Even with the expansion and attempts to speed up the development of the new jet bombers, the RAF had a serious gap in its front-line aircraft in the early 1950s. The swept-wing fighter was slow to come into service with the RAF. This was because a decision had been made (mistakenly as it turns out) that supersonic aircraft were 'too dangerous to warrant further research'. In 1946, the Director General of the Scientific Research (Air) said, 'The impression that supersonic aircraft are just around the corner is quite erroneous … the difficulties will be tackled by the use of rocket-driven motors. We do not have the heart to ask pilots to fly the high-speed models, so we shall make them radio-controlled.'

To bridge the gap, 430 Canadian-manufactured F-86 Sabres equipped Fighter Command and squadrons in Germany between 1950 and 1955, with Canada funding the airframes and the US providing the engines and other equipment. In addition, and by arrangement with the United States under the Atlantic Pact mutual arms aid agreement signed in Washington on 27 January 1950, 88 B-29 Superfortresses (renamed Washingtons) came into service with Bomber Command between 1950 and 1953. Fifty-two maritime reconnaissance Neptunes were also delivered for operations by four Coastal Command squadrons between 1952 and 1953.

After the Second World War, Britain constantly seemed to be involved in a conflict somewhere in the world. Just as the Berlin crisis broke, and the airlift began, Britain became deeply committed to a campaign in the Far East that was eventually to become a model for conducting counter-insurgency warfare. During the Japanese occupation of Malaya during the Second World War, the Allies had supplied arms, equipment and a few men to support the resistance war waged against the Japanese by the (mainly Chinese) Malayan Communist Party (MCP). At the end of the war, the communists had begun to exploit nationalist feelings throughout colonial South-East Asia and the MCP refused to hand back their weapons, retreating instead into the jungle to plan their next campaign. This was to free Malaya from British colonial rule. The MCP controlled a field army of insurgents, the Malayan Races Liberation Army (MRLA). The MRLA struck in 1948: terrorist attacks were made on rubber plantations and tin mines (the foundations of the Malayan economy), government property and civilians – both British and

Malay. A state of emergency was declared and Britain became involved in a campaign that would eventually run for twelve years – until 1960.

Operation Firedog was a civil and military campaign aimed at isolating the communist insurgents from the local support, which was vital to their survival. The very nature of this type of counter-insurgency warfare was exacerbated by the climate and terrain of Malaya, 70 per cent of which consists of jungle-covered mountains sparsely inhabited by indigenous peoples and linked only by jungle track and river. A variety of aircraft and helicopters were deployed to the area. In all thirty-one different basic types of aircraft in thirty-six versions were engaged in Operation Firedog.

Gradually the hold of the insurgents was broken and more and more areas were declared safe. Malaya became independent in 1957, although the emergency did not end until 1960. Operation Firedog finally brought peace and independence to Malaya and sustained its friendship with Britain.

Because of commitments in Malaya, Britain made only a limited contribution to the Korean War. The United Nations, largely at the instigation of the United States, decided to provide military support to the South Koreans when North Korea invaded them in June 1950. The North Koreans were defeated, but in the winter of 1950/51 Chinese communist army and air force intervention led to a bitter struggle and a stalemate around the 38th parallel (38° N latitude) until an armistice was agreed in July 1953. The RAF element of the British forces involved was limited to three squadrons of Sunderland flying boats for maritime reconnaissance patrols against seaborne incursions and movements around the coast. In addition, Hastings aircraft were involved in troop movements and casualty evacuations.

While the Malayan Emergency remained in progress, the RAF was called upon to participate in the emergency created in Kenya by the Mau Mau rebellion from 1952 to 1956. The RAF operated in a very similar role to that utilised in Malaya, but on a much-reduced scale. So scarce were RAF resources to support the ground troops that ageing Harvard trainers were equipped with Browning machine guns and eight 20lb anti-personnel bombs to go into action against the Mau Mau. The Harvards were successful and continued to play an important role throughout the four years of the emergency. They were supplemented by Bomber Command Avro Lincolns and ground-attack Vampire jets from Aden.

Having had a long-term interest in Egypt, the British withdrew forces in 1955, retaining stocks and an agreement for the use and defence of the critical Suez Canal. Under President Nasser, Egypt looked to the West for arms, but they refused. The Soviet Union stepped in, with a deal brokered by Czechoslovakia. As a consequence, the West withdrew its financial support for the construction of the economically essential Aswan High Dam. On 26 July 1956, Nasser nationalised the Suez Canal, which provided an economical route from Europe to the Far East, both in terms of time and money. In 1950, shipping was still the main method of moving supplies around the world.

On the day the Suez Canal was nationalised, the British Prime Minister, Sir Anthony Eden, asked the Chiefs of Staff to plan for a military intervention. Shortly afterwards, the French Prime Minister, Guy Mollet, suggested a joint operation and planning continued. Operation Musketeer, a British and French seaborne invasion supported by parachute forces to occupy the Canal Zone, was launched from Malta and Cyprus at the end of October. The RAF's task was to attack Egyptian airfields and prevent the Russian-built MiG-15 fighters and Il-28 bombers of the Egyptian Air Force from interfering with the invasion. Within two days, the Egyptian Air Force had effectively been put out of action. Canberras and Valiants were used for high-altitude precision bombing, while Canberras, Venoms and French fighter-bombers completed the destruction from low-level.

Both the seaborne and airborne assaults were successful. RAF Hastings and Valletta aircraft were used to drop British paratroops on to El Gamil airfield.

After seven days, a ceasefire was announced and United Nations forces took over in the Canal Zone. While the military operations were successful, they too had shown deficiencies in bombing techniques and base facilities; they had also emphasised the need to expand the air transport force.

Cyprus, as well as providing the main base for the launching of the Suez operations, was itself torn apart by a campaign of violence launched by EOKA guerrillas led by Colonel Georgios Grivas which started in 1956. The objective of EOKA was the unity of Cyprus with Greece. As in the Malayan conflict, the helicopter proved its worth in Cyprus – proving invaluable in supporting the ground forces hunting EOKA in the mountains. Sycamore helicopters from 284 Squadron pioneered the techniques of night flying and landing troops by abseiling down ropes from a hovering helicopter. In addition, the helicopters dropped food and ammunition, as well as providing casualty evacuation. The emergency ended in December 1959.

The 1950s was a period of immense technological advancement. At the beginning of 1950, the RAF was still utilising Second World War-era Avro Lincoln bombers, while Fighter Command still had propeller-driven Spitfires in its inventory. Jet fighters were on strength (and had been since 1944) but were limited to around 400mph by their straight wings and the relatively under-powered 1,700lb static thrust produced by the Welland 1 engine. By way of comparison with the jet performance, the propeller-driven Hawker Tempest II could still manage 440mph at 15,000ft while the Griffon-powered Spitfire PR.19 was good for 448mph at 26,000ft.

By 1959, things had changed dramatically. In just ten years Bomber Command had the Valiant, Vulcan, Victor and Canberra jet bombers in its inventory; some equipped with atomic weapons. The Avro Lincolns were long gone!

Transport Command had the ugly but effective Beverley and by 1959, the beautiful Bristol Britannia in its fleet.

Fighter Command had the Gloster Javelin, Supermarine Swift and Hawker Hunter – the latter pair capable of supersonic speed only in a dive. On 4 August 1954, the English Electric P.1A aircraft made its first flight at Boscombe Down with Wing Commander R.P. 'Bee' Beaumont at the controls. Within one year the aircraft had completed more than a hundred further test flights at supersonic speed. The P.1A was significantly re-engineered and re-engined with a pair of Rolls-Royce Avon 200 engines, providing a total thrust of over 20,000lbs. The P.1B, as the modified aircraft was designated, made its first flight on 4 April 1957. On 25 November 1958, XA847 became the first British aircraft ever to fly at Mach 2.0. The first full production aircraft entered service with the Central Fighter Establishment at Coltishall in December 1959, providing a fitting end to the decade. By the end of 1959, RAF strength had reduced to around 165,000 people (at 1950 it had been 193,100) and the total aircraft on strength had dropped to 5,194 (from 9,941 in 1950).

The 1948 inaugural 'Flying Display and Exhibition' was organised by the then Society of British Aircraft Constructors (SBAC) and accommodated nearly 200 exhibitors in two of the famous 'black sheds' at Farnborough. It succeeded eight SBAC meetings at other airfields near London. The first of these was in 1932, when the Royal Air Force allowed the 'New Types Park' (an enclave for prototypes) at its annual Hendon pageant to stay in place an extra day to enable foreign visitors to inspect the aircraft.

An innovation at the first Farnborough show in 1948 was public admission on two extra days to watch an enhanced air display. There were rows of aircraft parked on the north side of the current runway. British manufacturers were responsible for exhibiting the world's first civil jet airliner (the Rolls-Royce Nene-powered Vickers Viking), the first four-engined turbine-powered airliner (Vickers Viscount) and the first turboprop military trainer (Boulton Paul Balliol). They were all parked alongside the de Havilland 108, Europe's first supersonic jet.

In 1950, the SBAC adopted the show's current layout, with the crowd south of runway 07/25 (now 06/24) while the exhibition was moved to the end of runway 29, where today's static display begins. The show was an annual event and rapidly became *the* place to debut the latest aircraft. In the austere post-war years, celebrity status was afforded to Britain's test pilots, including Neville Duke, who came to the 1951 show in the Hawker P.1067 prototype just five weeks after its maiden flight at Boscombe Down on 20 July. The P.1067 became the successful Hunter fighter and ground-attack aircraft. Duke provided what one commentator described as 'the fastest flypasts ever seen by the British public' while displaying it.

Throughout the 1950s the SBAC Show at Farnborough produced surprises, many of which are documented and illustrated in the following chapters. British manufacturers showcased their latest civil and military designs at the show and it was usually the public's first sighting of the very latest aircraft – whatever the aircraft, it just *had* to be seen at Farnborough. The RAF also showcased their new in-service types and provided a suitable formation display team each year.

All images in this book have been provided from the archives of the Air Historical Branch – probably one of the best-kept secrets in aviation. Indeed, I am deeply indebted to Lee Barton, the branch's assistant photo archivist, who guided me through the various image archives and then provided much of the caption information from the branch's extensive and detailed records. The branch's individual image reference has been quoted in each case.

Sadly, little colour film existed in the early 1950s and what was available was expensive and often unreliable! As the years progressed, the availability of colour film increased, the price reduced and the amount of colour images created – many by the various RAF station photographers – increased significantly. That said, many of these priceless black and white images are historically significant and the lack of colour does not detract from their inclusion in this book.

Future volumes are planned in this series where colour illustrations will provide the very large majority of illustrations, especially for the post-1960 decades.

Keith Wilson
Ramsey, Cambridgeshire
September 2014

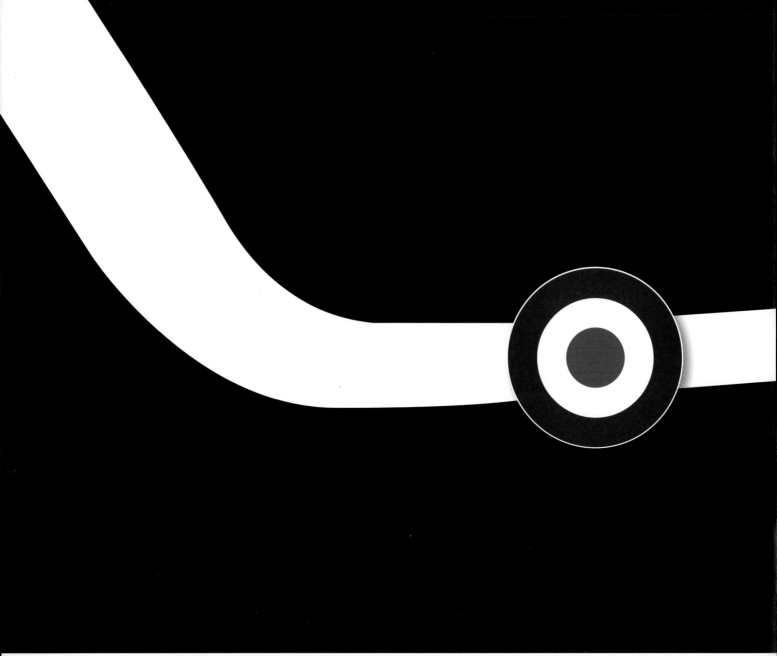

1950

At the beginning of 1950 and despite emerging from the Second World War as part of the victorious Allies, Britain was still enduring a period of rationing and severe austerity measures. The rationing of meat and all other foods would eventually continue until finally abolished on 4 July 1954.

On 23 February 1950 a General Election was held in the UK. The Conservative Party campaigned on a manifesto of ending rationing as quickly as possible; however, the Labour Party was returned with its majority badly slashed. On 26 May rationing of petrol finally ended.

The Royal Air Force was continuing to downsize – both in terms of people and aircraft – after its wartime efforts. At the conclusion of the Second World War, statistics indicate the RAF headcount stood at around 1.3 million, while the

total number of aircraft held on strength (including aircraft held in storage) was 61,584. By the start of 1950, more than a million men and women had been demobilised and the headcount had reduced to 193,100, while aircraft held on strength had reduced to 9,941 – a drop of almost 84 per cent on 1945 levels.

Λ The Boulton Paul P.111 experimental aircraft pictured at Pendeford airfield in May 1950. The aircraft was built to test the properties of delta-wing aircraft and could be fitted with a variety of wing-tip configurations for flight. The aircraft was completed at Boulton Paul's Wolverhampton factory but, as the grass runway at Pendeford was not suitable for operating the P.111, the aircraft was then dismantled and moved to Boscombe Down for flight testing (see also page 47). *(Crown Copyright/Air Historical Branch image ATP-19260b)*

Ⓐ Owing to the considerable commitments in Malaya, Britain only made a limited contribution to the UN efforts in Korea and was limited to three squadrons of Sunderland flying boats which began blockade operations off the west coast of Korea on 22 August 1950. Short Sunderland V, RN282/C, of 88 Squadron was photographed while participating in a daylight patrol along Korea's Yellow Sea Coast in October 1950. *(Crown Copyright/Air Historical Branch image CFP-248)*

Still at war?

Despite everyone's best efforts to operate in peace, the RAF was still involved in conflicts around the world. Britain was heavily committed in Malaya where Operation Firedog, a civil and military campaign aimed at isolating the communist insurgents, was under way. The conflict in Malaya was destined to continue until 1960.

In June 1950, when North Korea invaded South Korea, the United Nations decided to provide military assistance to South Korea, although largely at the United States' instigations. This conflict continued until an armistice was agreed in 1953. Owing to considerable commitments in Malaya, Britain only made a limited contribution to the UN efforts in Korea. The RAF contribution was limited to three squadrons of Sunderland flying boats, which began blockade operations off the west coast of Korea on 22 August

1950, and Hastings transport aircraft utilised in moving troops into theatre.

Southern Arabia from the Red Sea to Dhofar was subject to British influence from 1839, with Aden becoming a Crown Colony in 1937. In the hinterland there were constant inter-tribal conflicts, and in 1927, 8 Squadron was posted to the Aden Protectorate. Aden was an important British base because of its location both on the route to India and between East Africa and the Gulf, both spheres of British influence.

During the Second World War little attention was paid to tribal disputes, but in May 1945 the RAF returned to the area, where it was to remain for a number of years. The conflict continued into 1950. At the time, the RAF had Bristol Brigand B.1s of 8 Squadron, based at Khormaksar, involved in action against dissident tribesmen.

⋀ Members of the Argyll and Sutherland Highlanders boarding the first Hastings aircraft to leave RAF Lyneham, Wiltshire, for Japan on 19 September 1950. The troops were reinforcements for British forces in Korea. *(Crown Copyright/Air Historical Branch image PRB-1-931)*

⋁ A line-up of No 60 Squadron Supermarine Spitfire FR.18s in less-than-ideal conditions at an RAF airfield in Malaya, 13 November 1950. No 60 Squadron had taken the Spitfire FR.18 on charge in March 1950 and they only remained with the unit until shortly after this photograph was taken. *(Crown Copyright/Air Historical Branch image CFP-289)*

Bridging the gap

In January 1947, a decision taken by the then Labour Government to create a strategic nuclear force led to the largest ever peacetime spend on the UK defence budget, when a planned amount of £4,700 million was allocated over the three years from 1951–4. By comparison, the defence budget for 1950 was a paltry £800 million. That strike force would take nearly ten years to finally bring to fruition and was exacerbated by the confrontational situation in Europe during the Cold War, along with the shooting war in Korea. A large short-term capability gap became apparent in the RAF inventory – particularly in regard to swept-wing fighters, maritime patrol aircraft and long-range heavy bombers.

To provide suitable equipment for Fighter Command and squadrons in Germany, 430 Canadian-built F-86 Sabre aircraft were acquired after arrangement with the United States, but these did not start arriving until January 1953. To cover the maritime reconnaissance role, fifty-two Neptunes – all former US Navy P2V-5s – were operated by four Coastal Command squadrons between 1952 and 1953, prior to the arrival of the Avro Shackleton.

On 1 August 1950, the first Boeing Washingtons entered service with 115 Squadron at RAF Marham, as a stop-gap measure to fill the long-range bomber requirements during the Cold War. Initially seventy of the former USAF B-29s and B-29As were ordered, but this was later increased to eighty-eight. All had been in cocooned storage before being modernised for use by the RAF. Many of the Washingtons were subsequently replaced in RAF service by Canberra aircraft by 1954, but a number did continue to serve the RAF until early 1958.

Norwegian–British–Swedish Antarctic Expedition

The Norwegian–British–Swedish expedition of 1949–52 was the first in Antarctica to involve an international team of scientists. Its base was located on the coast of Dronning Maud Land – an area lying between the meridians of 20°W and 45°E which was territory annexed by Norway just before the Second World War. Apart from surveys and mapping, the main objective was to carry out a wide-ranging programme of scientific

➤ VX127, one of two Auster AOP.6s used by the British Antarctic Flight, pictured on board the MV *Norsel* during the voyage south from Cape Town in late December 1949/early January 1950. The aircraft were initially stored in packing cases and then assembled while in the South African port. Fitted with either floats or skis, both Auster aircraft were used to carry out a series of reconnaissance flights as the party approached the Antarctic to locate sites suitable for setting up a base camp for the Norwegian–British–Swedish Antarctic Expedition. Once the camp had been set up, the aircraft carried out a series of survey flights over Queen Maud Land and were also employed on resupply missions to and from the *Norsel*. The expedition set sail on the return voyage to Cape Town on 20 February 1950, and upon arrival in South Africa, both VX127 and VX126 were handed over to the local RAF Liaison Officer for disposal. *(Crown Copyright/Air Historical Branch image PRB-1-606)*

Λ The leader of the RAF Antarctic Flight, Squadron Leader G.B. Walford, with one of the two Auster AOP.6 aircraft used during the Norwegian–British–Swedish Antarctic Expedition of 1949/50. *(Crown Copyright/Air Historical Branch image PRB-1-620)*

investigations with particular interest in discovering whether climatic fluctuations similar to those observed in the Arctic were also occurring in Antarctica. In terms of the expedition, Norway was mainly responsible for meteorology and topographical surveys, Britain for geology and Sweden for glaciology.

In addition to the scientific team, a small five-man RAF group, together with two light Auster aircraft (VX126 and VX127) used by the British Antarctic Flight accompanied the expedition on the MV *Norsel*. Fitted with either floats or skis, both Auster aircraft were used to carry out a series of reconnaissance flights as the party approached the Antarctic to locate sites suitable to set up base camp. Once the camp had been set up, the two aircraft carried out a series of survey flights over Queen Maud Land and were also employed on resupply missions to and from the *Norsel*.

At readiness

'In the austere days of 1950, the concentration of nine fighter squadrons on one RAF airfield was a spectacle to gladden the hearts of the air-minded,' was how *Flight* magazine reported a joint exercise at RAF Horsham St Faith involving both Royal Auxiliary Air Force (RAuxAF) and regular squadrons in March 1950. Five units visited the

base: fifteen Spitfire F.22s representing Nos 610 (County of Chester) and 613 (City of Manchester) Squadrons; four Vampire F.1s were supplied by 605 (County of Warwick) Squadron; 616 (South Yorkshire) Squadron brought six Meteor F.3s and a single T.7; and 504 (County of Nottingham) Squadron, the first Auxiliary unit to receive the Meteor F.4s, had five aircraft assembled. A security ban had precluded *Flight* from recording the identity of the resident squadrons at Horsham St Faith, but these can now be confirmed as 43, 74, 234 and 245 Squadrons, all operating the Meteor F.4.

Despite the title 'Auxiliary', the weekend squadrons were part of Britain's front-line air defence and in war would have assumed equal combatant status alongside the Regular component. A logical step was taken in the summer of 1949 when all twenty Auxiliary fighter squadrons were integrated within Fighter Command. Shortly afterwards, each Auxiliary squadron was affiliated to a Regular counterpart.

Flight magazine's report continued, 'For the occasion, the weather was perfect: a brilliant sun, and sufficient cloud to give realism to ground-controlled interceptions. Almost every defending force attacked its quarry successfully at heights up to 28,000 feet, and commanders were extremely satisfied with practice gained and lessons learned.'

▲ Fighters from three Royal Auxiliary Air Force squadrons pictured at RAF Horsham St Faith, Norfolk, on 16 March 1950, during an exercise for regular and reserve squadrons. In the foreground are two Spitfire F.22s (PK554/RAQ-A and PK577/RAQ-D) of 610 (County of Chester) RAuxAF Squadron, based at Hooton Park, Liverpool. Three Vampire F.1s of 601 (County of London) RAuxAF Squadron (coded 'RAL') and Meteor F.3s of 616 (South Yorkshire) RAuxAF Squadron (coded 'RAW') complete the line-up. *(Crown Copyright/Air Historical Branch image PRB-1-30)*

▼ Groundcrew from 504 (County of Nottingham) Royal Auxiliary Air Force Squadron manhandle one of their Gloster Meteor F.4s, VW274, on the flightline at RAF Horsham St Faith, Norfolk, during a combined exercise held at the fighter station in March 1950. *(Crown Copyright/Air Historical Branch image PRB-1-23)*

Groundcrew from 605 (County of Warwick) Royal Auxiliary Air Force Squadron refuel and carry out final checks on Vampire F.1, TG348/RAL-B, in preparation for another training sortie from RAF Horsham St Faith, Norfolk, during a combined regular and reserve fighter squadron exercise held in March 1950. *(Above: Crown Copyright/Air Historical Branch image PRB-1-26 ; below: Crown Copyright/Air Historical Branch image PRB 1-33)*

Λ The prototype English Electric Canberra, VN799, pictured during a test flight in April 1950. VN799 made its first flight on 13 May 1949 and caused a sensation at that year's Farnborough Air Show when English Electric's chief test pilot, Roly Beamont, performed a series of steep turns and a half-loop during his display. However, not everything went as planned. During a low pass along the runway, Beamont opened the bomb bay doors only to be informed by his co-pilot that his instrumentation had fallen out of the aircraft – a fact confirmed in a radio message from air traffic control. Some of Beamont's engine instruments also malfunctioned and the aircraft was landed and taxied away from public view for further investigation. *(Crown Copyright/Air Historical Branch image PRB-1-117)*

V Flight Lieutenant G. Hulse of the Central Flying School taxiing at RAF North Weald on 15 May 1950 for an aerobatic display in his Boulton Paul Balliol T.2, VR593/FDL-O. Hulse was competing against a Spitfire LF.XVIe flown by Pilot Officer I.K. Posta from No 17 Squadron for the privilege of displaying at the forthcoming Farnborough Air Show. The competition was declared a tie, but the Czech pilot in his Spitfire edged out Hulse for the right to fly his routine at the September event. *(Crown Copyright/Air Historical Branch image PRB-1-263)*

◄ Pilots of 613 (City of Manchester) Squadron Royal Auxiliary Air Force being briefed by their Commanding Officer, Squadron Leader J.B. Wales, next to one of the unit's Spitfire F.22s at RAF North Weald on 3 June 1950. Some of the pilots wear the rank of 'Pilot 1' – three stars within a wreath under an RAF Eagle – which was the equivalent of Sergeant Pilot. These unpopular non-commissioned ranks were abolished in 1950 and non-commissioned aircrew reverted to the traditional ranks. *(Crown Copyright/Air Historical Branch image PRB-1-358)*

▼ Gloster Meteor F.4s of 226 Operational Conversion Unit at RAF Stradishall, Norfolk, in June 1950. This photograph was taken shortly before four aircraft from the unit displayed at the Orly Air Display near Paris on 11 June. The aircraft wear two different sets of codes; 'HX' being No 1 (Gunnery) Squadron, while 'KR'-coded aircraft are flown by No 2 Tactical Squadron. *(Crown Copyright/Air Historical Branch image PRB-1-368)*

➤ Gloster Meteor T.7, VW418, in flight, showing the heavily framed cockpit of the trainer version of the Meteor. Issued in February 1949 to the Empire Central Flying School at RAF Hullavington, Wiltshire, the aircraft was then transferred to the Ministry of Supply at Boscombe Down for trials work. *(Crown Copyright/ Air Historical Branch image PRB-1-578)*

⋁ The prototype de Havilland Venom fighter/bomber aircraft, VV612, pictured during a test flight. Originally designated as the Vampire 8, the new aircraft featured a revised, thinner wing, which could be fitted with under-wing and wing-tip tanks to carry additional fuel for the de Havilland Ghost engine, which developed 40 per cent more power than the Vampire's Goblin. Over 1,000 Venoms were produced for the RAF and Royal Navy, serving between 1952 and 1962. Note the solid canopy fitted. *(Crown Copyright/Air Historical Branch image PRB-1-591)*

Bristol Brigand TF/F.1, RH747, in flight during 1950. RH747 was one of thirteen early Brigands built in 1946 as torpedo-bomber/fighters and it remained with the manufacturer for trials before joining the Aircraft Torpedo Development Unit at Gosport in November 1950. *(Crown Copyright/Air Historical Branch image PRB-1-735)*

◄ A de Havilland Mosquito PR.34, VL619, photographed in flight from its base at Fayid, Egypt, while serving with 13 Squadron during 1950. VL619 joined 13 Squadron late in 1949 and served until 1951. *(Crown Copyright/Air Historical Branch image PRB-1-753)*

△ Avro Anson C.19, VM368, of 58 Squadron, photographed in flight in mid-1950. The unit was one of a number of Bomber Command photo-reconnaissance squadrons based at RAF Benson flying Mosquito PR.34s, while the Anson was used for communications and light transport duties. *(Crown Copyright/Air Historical Branch image PRB-1-806)*

➤ Vickers Viking C.1, VL272, of the Transport Command Development Unit (TCDU) at RAF Abingdon. VL272 joined the TCDU in September 1948 before being transferred to 240 OCU (Operational Conversion Unit) in February 1951. *(Crown Copyright/Air Historical Branch image PRB-1-811)*

The prototype Vickers Varsity aircrew trainer, VX828, in flight during 1950. The Varsity was developed from the Valetta and had a tricycle undercarriage, longer wings and increased range which permitted training flights to be undertaken as far afield as Malta, Cyprus and North Africa. The bulge under the fuselage was the student bomb-aimer's position and up to twenty-four 25lb practice bombs could also be carried. The Varsity was also fitted with the H2S navigation radar used by Bomber Command aircraft of the time, such as the Avro Lincoln. In the training role, the Varsity replaced the Wellington from late 1951 and served with a number of flying training and air navigation schools until mid-1976 when the type was replaced by the Handley Page/Scottish Aviation Jetstream T.1. *(Crown Copyright/Air Historical Branch image PRB-1-816)*

Vickers Viking C.2, VL248, pictured while flying with The King's Flight at RAF Benson. The aircraft, which served with the flight from January 1947 to May 1955, was fitted out with workshop and maintenance equipment in support of the other VIP passenger Vikings of The King's Flight. *(Crown Copyright/Air Historical Branch image PRB-1-829)*

The third prototype Boulton Paul Balliol T.2 trainer, VW899, photographed in 1950. The Balliol only served in the training role with 7 Flying Training School at Cottesmore and the RAF College Cranwell for a short period of time (1952–5), owing to the emergence of jet training aircraft, but a few survived as communications aircraft and instructional airframes until 1961. A Balliol destined for the Ceylon Air Force was the final aircraft built by Boulton Paul in mid-1957. *(Crown Copyright/Air Historical Branch image PRB-1-814)*

Short Sunderland V, SZ568/TA-C, of 235 Operational Conversion Unit based at Calshot, photographed in 1950. SZ568 remained with 235 OCU when it was redesignated as the Flying Boat Training Squadron at Pembroke Dock on October 1953 and served until October 1956 when it was struck off. *(Crown Copyright/Air Historical Branch image PRB-1-858)*

De Havilland Chipmunk T.10, WB555, of Oxford University Air Squadron, based at Kidlington airport, near Oxford, is seen here in 1950. *(Crown Copyright/Air Historical Branch image PRB-1-871)*

Two views of Avro Athena T.2, VR567, of the RAF Flying College at RAF Manby, photographed in 1950. The Athena was the losing design in a competition for a two-seat advanced trainer held in 1948/9, which was won by the Boulton Paul Balliol. Eleven Athena T.2s served at Manby between 1950 and 1955. *(Above: Crown Copyright/Air Historical Branch image PRB-1-859; right: Crown Copyright/Air Historical Branch image PRB-1-862)*

⋎ De Havilland Vampire FB.5, VV472/J5-J, of 3 Squadron based at Gütersloh, Germany, photographed on 19 July 1950. At the time, the squadron was part of the British Air Forces of Occupation (BAFO) – the 2nd Tactical Air Force did not come into existence until returning to its pre-BAFO title on 1 September 1951. *(Crown Copyright/Air Historical Branch image CLP-322)*

Two de Havilland Vampire FB.5s of 6 Squadron (with VX981/K, nearest the camera), kick up a dust cloud as they take off from the desert airstrip at Mafraq in Jordan on 1 August 1950. The aircraft were taking part in a month-long detachment from Deversoir, Egypt. *(Crown Copyright/Air Historical Branch image CMP-154)*

Seven de Havilland Vampire FB.5s of 6 Squadron taking off in line-abreast formation from the desert airstrip at Mafraq, Jordan, on 1 August 1950. *(Crown Copyright/Air Historical Branch image CMP-155)*

First flight for Supermarine Type 528

The Supermarine Type 528, VV119, made its first flight in March 1950. The aircraft was based on the Fleet Air Arm jet, the Supermarine Attacker, but had swept wings and a swept fin fitted – although it still had what appeared to be an antiquated tailwheel undercarriage configuration. The aircraft was significantly modified (including the fitting of tricycle undercarriage) and re-emerged as the Type 535 in August that year. This aircraft was the forerunner of the Supermarine Swift family of fighters which equipped four squadrons of the RAF – Nos 2, 4, 56 and 79 – between February 1954 and March 1961.

VV129 was also the star of the 1952 film, *The Sound Barrier*, in the guise of 'Prometheus'.

Operation Musgrave

On 20 March 1950, a number of Avro Lincoln B.2B bombers of No 57 Squadron were deployed to Tengah airfield, Singapore, as part of Operation Musgrave. Six days later, eight of the aircraft were involved in dropping 1,000lb (450kg) bombs on a terrorist base in Malaya. No 57 Squadron were supplemented at Tengah in June 1950 by Lincoln B.2Bs of 100 Squadron and 61 Squadron aircraft in December. No 57 Squadron remained at Tengah until July 1951.

First operational British helicopter

The first British operational helicopter unit, the Casualty Evacuation Flight (CEF), was formed at Seletar, Singapore, on 1 May 1950, with Dragonfly HC.2 helicopters to provide jungle rescue capabilities. The Dragonfly HC.2 was equipped with accommodation for two stretcher cases in closed panniers on each side of the fuselage. The role of the CEF was expanded to form No 194 Squadron – the very first helicopter squadron in the RAF.

Swept-wing jet on HMS *Illustrious*

Although Lieutenant Commander Eric 'Winkle' Brown had landed a specially modified de Havilland Vampire, LZ551/G, onto HMS *Ocean* during trials on 3 December 1945, the Supermarine Type 510, VV106, became the very first swept-wing jet aircraft to land and take off from an aircraft carrier during trials on HMS *Illustrious* on 8 November 1950.

The first of two experimental Supermarine 510 aircraft, VV106, in flight. Built to meet Specification E38/46 (and in competition with the Hawker P.1052), the aircraft was a development of the Royal Navy's Attacker fighter and was the first British jet aircraft to feature a swept wing and tailplane. Despite its futuristic look, the Type 510 retained the Attacker's tail-dragger undercarriage and was not capable of supersonic flight, mainly because of the relatively low power of its Nene turbojet engine. On 8 November 1950, VV106 became the first jet aircraft in the world to land and take off from an aircraft carrier when undergoing trials on HMS *Illustrious*. The design was ultimately developed into the Swift, which served with RAF fighter squadrons between 1954 and 1961. *(Crown Copyright/Air Historical Branch image PRB-1-874)*

Hawker Tempest V, SN329, pictured after being converted for the target-towing role and fitted with underwing winches. Delivered in November 1945 to 80 Squadron, SN329 was damaged in a flying accident and returned to Hawker for rebuild, reappearing as the prototype Tempest TT.5 in late 1948. After trials at Boscombe Down, it was returned for further modifications before joining the Airborne Forces Experimental Establishment at Beaulieu in mid-1950. In May 1952, SN329 was issued to the Armament Practice Camp at Sylt in Germany, but suffered an accident just two weeks later which resulted in the aircraft being written off. *(Crown Copyright/Air Historical Branch image PRB-1-922)*

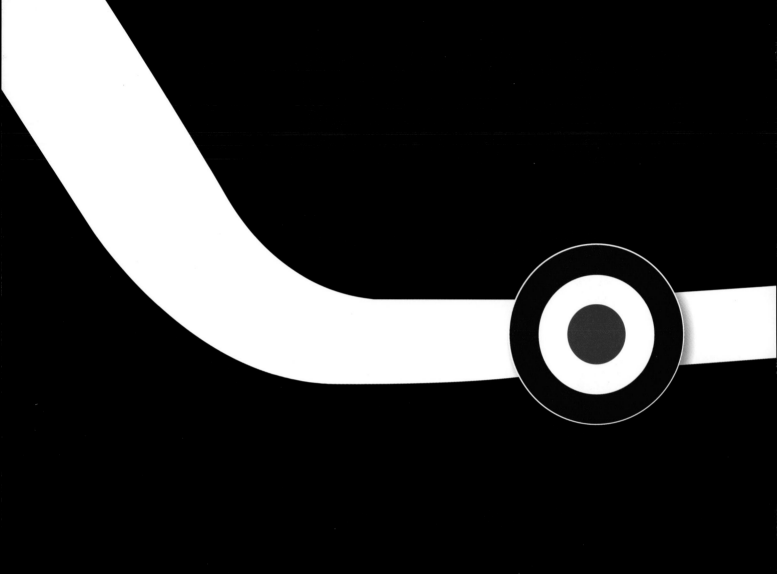

1951

The 1950 General Election had given the Labour Party a greatly reduced parliamentary majority – a mere five seats compared to the triple-digit majority they had enjoyed five years earlier. The mediocre result was blamed on post-war austerity measures, which dented Labour's appeal to middle-class voters. Clement Attlee's second term was tame compared to his first.

By 1951, the Attlee Government was exhausted – with several of its most important ministers ailing, aging or gone – and no one representing new ideas. The party fatally split in 1951 over an austerity budget brought in by the Chancellor, Hugh Gaitskell, to pay for the cost of Britain's participation in the Korean War. Aneurin 'Nye' Bevan resigned in protest against the new charges for 'teeth and spectacles' introduced by that budget, and was joined in this action by several ministers, including the future Prime Minister Harold Wilson.

Finding it impossible to govern, Attlee called a general election for 25 October 1951, hoping to achieve a more workable majority. However, Labour went on to lose the election to Churchill's renewed and reinvigorated Conservatives.

Attlee's term as Prime Minister, which lasted six years and ninety-two days, was the longest unbroken time spent by any Labour leader as Prime Minister until the premiership of Tony Blair more than fifty years later.

The subsequent Labour defeat was significant for several reasons: the party polled almost a quarter of a million votes more than the Tories and their National Liberal allies combined; they gained the highest number of votes that Labour had ever won (and has ever won as of 2013), and won the most votes of any political party in any election in British political history – a record only surpassed in 1992. Despite this, it was the Conservatives who formed the next government with a majority of one. Lord De L'Isle and Dudley VC was the new Secretary of State for Air, and, as far as the Royal Air Force was concerned, the object was to increase the spend on the front line in all theatres and in particular to expand the forces placed under the Supreme Allied Commander, Europe, to provide more modern aircraft, and to overhaul the defence radar network of the UK.

▼ One of the first publicity shots of the Hawker Hunter prototype, WB188 (note the 'SECRET' classification), taken around
time of the aircraft's first flight at Boscombe Down on 20 July 1951. The Hunter was to become Fighter Command's standard
day fighter in the second half of the 1950s, with over 1,000 aircraft in five versions equipping squadrons throughout the service.
(Crown Copyright/Air Historical Branch image ATP-21301c)

HAWKER F 3/48
AVON
JULY 1951

A line-up of Meteor F.8s from 92 Squadron at RAF Horsham St Faith on 10 January 1951. The F.8 variant of the Meteor was first issued to 245 Squadron (also based at Horsham St Faith) at the end of June 1950 and it became the standard day fighter used by Fighter Command, serving with twenty front-line squadrons and ten Auxiliary Air Force squadrons. Positioned further along the line-up are a number of Meteor F.4s from the Duxford-based 66 Squadron. *(Crown Copyright/Air Historical Branch image PRB-1-1461)*

The Right Honourable R.G. Menzies, the Australian Prime Minister, releases a bottle of Australian champagne during a ceremony held at Biggin Hill on 19 January 1951, in which he officially named the first English Electric Canberra jet bomber, WD929. The event was followed by a flight demonstration by English Electric's Chief Test Pilot, Roly Beamont, and lunch at the Savoy in London. The first English Electric Canberra aircraft joined 101 Squadron at RAF Binbrook, Lincolnshire, in May 1951, and the very last aircraft – Canberra PR9s of 39 Squadron – served until they were finally retired from service in July 2006. *(Crown Copyright/Air Historical Branch image PRB-1-1484)*

English Electric Canberra B.2 comes into service

Famous as the first jet bomber to be produced in Britain and the first to serve with the RAF, the prototype Canberra (VN799) made its first flight at Warton on 13 May 1949, with Wing Commander Roland 'Bee' Beamont at the controls. In the Mosquito tradition, the aircraft was unarmed and relied on high speed to escape fighters. The low-aspect ratio wing was chosen to provide maximum fuel economy at the highest possible cruising altitude and also provided the aircraft with remarkable manoeuvrability.

Originally intended for radar bombing with a crew of two, the Canberra was changed at the fifth prototype (VX165) to B.2 standard with visual aiming in the nose and a crew of three. The first B.2 flew on 23 April 1950, and the first production aircraft (WD929) flew on 8 October 1950. The B.2 version entered service with No 101 Squadron at RAF Binbrook in May 1951. Canberras were ordered in large quantities and built at four factories by English Electric, Short Brothers, Avro and Handley Page. Production of the B.2 version totalled 416 aircraft.

➤ A striking head-on view of one of the first Canberra B.2s to serve with the RAF, taken in early 1951. Of the three-man crew, only the pilot, seated on the left-hand side of the cockpit, had any real view of the outside world. The navigator and bomb-aimer sat at consoles within the fuselage of the aircraft – the two small skylight panels immediately behind the cockpit bubble being the only clue to their positions. In the event of a visual bomb-drop, the bomb-aimer would move forward to lie prone in the nose and use a secondary bomb sight. *(Crown Copyright/Air Historical Branch image PRB-1-1596)*

◤ The scene at the English Electric factory in early 1951 with the first three production Canberra B.2s – WD929, WD930 and WD931 – along with VN828, the third prototype, lined up with an Avro Lincoln B.2 of 101 Squadron. The Lincoln B.2 would give way to the Canberra in May 1951 when 101 Squadron at RAF Binbrook, Lincolnshire, became the RAF's first jet bomber squadron. *(Crown Copyright/Air Historical Branch image PRB-1-1600)*

➤ The fifth prototype Canberra, VX165, was converted to become the first aircraft modified to B.2 standard. First flown in April 1950, VX165 is seen here in March 1951 with the transparent visual aiming nose and an additional position for a third crew member. It was powered by a pair of Rolls-Royce Avon 101s, which became the standard for production B.2 variants. *(Crown Copyright/Air Historical Branch image PRB-1-1757)*

V Groundcrew fix a cargo pannier to a Handley Page Halifax during a combined air/land exercise held at RAF Watchfield in **March 1951.** *(Crown Copyright/Air Historical Branch image PRB-1-1771)*

Boeing Washington B.1 bombers of 115 Squadron, based at RAF Marham, are seen here during a training flight to the RAF bombing range at Heligoland, Germany, on 27 February 1951. Bomber Command took delivery of eighty-eight B-29 Superfortresses from the US Air Force under the American military aid programme for Europe. All of the aircraft were former USAF B-29 and B-29As taken out of 'cocooned' storage and modernised before reaching operational status. Bomber Command had suffered drastic reductions in strength after the war, and its long-range strike force was limited to relatively few squadrons of Avro Lincolns. The arrival of the jet-powered four-engine V-bombers was some way off. The first of these, the Vickers Valiant, arrived with 230 OCU at RAF Gaydon in early 1955. Most of the Washington aircraft had returned to the USA by mid-1954, but a few remained in service with 192 Squadron in 90 Group, based at RAF Watton, Norfolk, until 1958. *(Above: Crown Copyright/Air Historical Branch image PRB-1-1655; below: Crown Copyright/Air Historical Branch image PRB-1-1658)*

A trainee pilot at 203 Advanced Flying School, RAF Driffield, undergoing ejection seat training on 11 April 1951. The training rig, designed by Martin Baker, reproduced the sensations of an in-flight ejection and rapidly propelled the seat to a height of 30ft. *(Above: Crown Copyright/Air Historical Branch image PRB-1-1871; right: Crown Copyright/Air Historical Branch image PRB-1-1874)*

Handley Page Hastings Met.1, TG616, photographed in April 1951, shortly after conversion by the manufacturer to its weather reconnaissance role. After joining 511 Squadron as a standard transport aircraft in January 1950, TG616 was returned to Handley Page for conversion in November. Following the completion of the work, the aircraft was transferred to 5 Maintenance Unit in April 1951 and remained in store until returned to C.1 standard in late 1954 to fly with 53/99 Squadrons at RAF Lyneham. Further service with Nos 114 and 36 Squadrons at nearby RAF Colerne followed, until the aircraft was transferred to training duties with 242 Operational Conversion Unit at RAF Dishforth in September 1961. In 1967, TG616 was withdrawn from use and moved to RAF Marham for firefighting practice. *(Crown Copyright/Air Historical Branch image PRB-1-1955)*

The first de Havilland Vampire two-seat trainer – still wearing its 'B' class registration of G-5-7 – pictured at RAF Driffield while undergoing trials with 203 Advanced Flying School in April 1951. The aircraft was selected as the standard RAF advanced trainer in the following year, replacing the piston-engined Harvard. *(Crown Copyright/Air Historical Branch image PRB-1-1965)*

Air gunners training at the Central Gunnery School at RAF Leconfield are briefed by their instructor before a sortie in one of the school's Avro Lincoln B.IIs, RF396, in April 1951. *(Crown Copyright/Air Historical Branch image PRB-1-1987)*

Gloster Meteor F.4s and personnel of 600 (City of London) Squadron, Royal Auxiliary Air Force, parade at Biggin Hill on 16 April 1951 for an official visit by the Secretary of State for Air, Mr Arthur Henderson. The squadron, along with fellow Biggin Hill-based 615 (County of Surrey) Squadron RAuxAF, were among ten auxiliary units called up for three months' full-time service with Fighter Command. *(Crown Copyright/Air Historical Branch image PRB-1-2089)*

Farewell to the Mosquito

The final flight made by a de Havilland Mosquito aircraft in RAF service occurred at West Malling on 30 April 1951, when 85 Squadron Mosquito NF.36, RL348, took off for the final meteorological reconnaissance flight by the type. The pilot was Flight Lieutenant J.H. Corre and the navigator Flight Lieutenant R. McFarlin. The event took place just four months after the last of 7,781 Mosquito aircraft was delivered to the RAF. The aircraft in this case, VX916, was immediately placed in storage at 48 Maintenance Unit at Hawarden, Cheshire, and later sold to the Yugoslav Air Force in December 1951.

◁ The two-man crew of de Havilland Mosquito NF.36, RL148, prepare to board their aircraft at West Malling, Kent, for the final meteorological reconnaissance flight by the type in RAF service, 30 April 1951. The pilot was Flight Lieutenant J.H. Corre and the navigator Flight Lieutenant R. McFarlin, both flying with 85 Squadron. This event took place just four months after the last of 7,781 Mosquito aircraft was delivered to the RAF. The aircraft in this case, VX916, was immediately placed in storage at 48 Maintenance Unit at Hawarden and was later sold to the Yugoslav Air Force in December 1951. *(Crown Copyright/Air Historical Branch image PRB-1-2185)*

▽ Gloster Meteor F.8s of 74 Squadron, based at RAF Horsham St Faith, photographed in flight over East Anglia on 3 May 1951. The four aircraft are WA874/4D-K, VZ540/4D-I, VZ512/4D-D and VZ547/4D-B. *(Crown Copyright/Air Historical Branch image PRB-1-2193)*

➤ Four de Havilland Chipmunk T.10s of 18 Reserve Flying School are seen here flying along England's south coast on 17 May 1951, during a sortie from Fairoaks airport. The aircraft, WB629/22, WB628/RCT-T, WB622/16 and WB634/27, wear a mixture of four-letter and numerical codes. *(Crown Copyright/Air Historical Branch image PRB-1-2296)*

⋎ The Supermarine Type 535 experimental fighter, VV119, photographed in flight in 1951. First flown as the Type 528 in March 1950, the aircraft underwent a series of modifications (including the fitting of a tricycle undercarriage in place of the tail-dragger configuration originally installed) and re-emerged as the Type 535 in August 1950. This aircraft was the forerunner to the Swift family of fighters flown by four squadrons of the RAF – Nos 2, 4, 56 and 79 – between February 1954 and March 1961. *(Crown Copyright/Air Historical Branch image PRB-1-2900)*

The first prototype Vickers Type 660, WB210, photographed around the time of the aircraft's first flight in May 1951. The aircraft was lost during a test flight on 12 January 1952, when a fire broke out in the port wing. Development of this type continued and it eventually entered RAF service as the Valiant B.1 with 138 Squadron at Gaydon, Warwickshire, in 1955, thus becoming the first of the RAF's so-called 'V-Force' of four-engined nuclear bombers (see also page 85). *(Crown Copyright/Air Historical Branch image PRB-1-2384)*

The Boulton Paul P.111 delta-wing research aircraft, VT935, pictured during a test flight from Boscombe Down in 1951. Over the three years of the programme, the P.111 suffered a number of relatively minor mishaps. The substantially modified aircraft was rechristened the P.111A. The aircraft's final flight was on 20 June 1958. The airframe is now exhibited at the Midland Air Museum, Coventry (see also pages 14 and 15). *(Crown Copyright/Air Historical Branch image PRB-1-2473)*

In June 1956, 74 Squadron was selected to fly a formation aerobatic display at the Paris Air Show. Four of the squadron's Meteor F.8s (WA838/F, WA824/S, VZ557/N and VZ544/Z) are seen here during rehearsals for their appearance, three of which are wearing the unit's famous 'tiger' markings. *(Crown Copyright/Air Historical Branch image PRB-1-2493)*

Members of 201 Squadron launch one of the unit's Sunderland GR.5 flying boats, PP117/A-W, from the slipway at Pembroke Dock, 29 June 1951. At this time, the squadron was preparing for their forthcoming two-month tour of the West Indies and the USA. *(Crown Copyright/Air Historical Branch image PRB-1-2678)*

A Westland Dragonfly HC.2 lands in a clearing in the Malayan jungle marked with pieces of white cloth during a demonstration of air casualty evacuation on 30 June 1951. The casualty is carried in the external pannier. The aircraft is WF311, one of three Dragonfly helicopters used by the Far East Air Force for trials in Malaya between 1950 and 1952. *(Above: Crown Copyright/Air Historical Branch image CFP-467; below: Crown Copyright/Air Historical Branch image CFP-476)*

The pilots of five Hawker Hurricanes of the Portuguese Air Force being greeted on their arrival at RAF Tangmere on 16 July 1951. The five aircraft were to be used in a forthcoming Battle of Britain film, *Angels One-Five*. *(Above: Crown Copyright/Air Historical Branch image PRB-1-2853; below: Crown Copyright/Air Historical Branch image PRB-1-2857)*

Vickers Type 660's first flight

The first prototype Vickers Type 660, WB210, made its first flight in May 1951. The aircraft was destroyed in an accident during a test flight over Hampshire on 12 January 1952 when an uncontrollable fire started in the port wing. Development continued with the second prototype (WB215) which first flew in April 1952. The type eventually entered RAF service as the Valiant B.1 with 138 Squadron at Gaydon, Warwickshire, in 1955, thus becoming the first of the RAF's so-called 'V-Force' of four-engined nuclear bombers.

The Vickers Valiant prototype, WB210, photographed during a test flight in mid-1951 (see also page 47). *(Crown Copyright/Air Historical Branch image PRB-1-2905)*

Flying over the North Pole

In July 1951, a crew from RAF Manby made a pair of long-range navigational flights in a specially modified Avro Lincoln B.2, RE367, named *Aries III*. The first was from Keflavik, Iceland, to Eielson Air Force Base in Alaska over the Geographic North Pole. The return flight from Alaska to RAF Manby took them over the Magnetic North Pole. The modified Lincoln B.2 was fitted with the nose of a Lancastrian (sometimes referred to as a Lincolnian), and was the third of five *Aries* aircraft used by the RAF on a series of long-range navigation flights.

∀ The crew of Avro Lincoln RE367 *Aries III* pose with their aircraft at RAF Manby after flying over the Geographic North Pole during a flight between Keflavik, Iceland, and Eielson Air Force Base in Alaska; and across the Magnetic North Pole during the return flight from Alaska to Manby in July 1951. Pictured second from the left is the Lincoln's co-pilot, Wing Commander A.H. Humphrey, who was later Marshal of the Royal Air Force, Chief of the Air Staff between 1974 and 1976 and Chief of the Defence Staff from October 1976 to January 1977. *(Crown Copyright/Air Historical Branch image PRB-1-3012)*

⚠ In 1946, a new system of coding for aircraft in Flying Training, Technical Training and Reserve Commands was introduced, which comprised a four-letter code. The first letter (F, R or T) stood for the Command, the second and third letters denoted the unit, and the fourth identified the individual aircraft. Five Harvard IIBs of 3 Flying Training School based at RAF Feltwell (including FS756/FBT-Z, FX245/FBT-W and KF911/FBT-T) are photographed here in starboard echelon formation in September 1951 while displaying the new coding system. *(Crown Copyright/Air Historical Branch image PRB-1-3242)*

Overseas conflicts

At the beginning of 1951, Britain was still involved with emergencies in Malaya and Korea. To make matters worse, serious internal security problems arose in the Suez Canal Zone, which would eventually lead to the Suez Crisis in 1956.

In 1922, Britain gave nominal independence to Egypt, but it was some years before an agreement was reached. The Anglo-Egyptian Treaty, signed in London in 1936, proclaimed Egypt to be an independent sovereign state, but allowed for British troops to continue to be stationed in the Suez Canal Zone to protect Britain's financial and strategic interest in the canal. This was to be the case until 1956, at which time the need for their presence would be re-examined and, if necessary, renegotiated.

After the Second World War there was an upsurge of nationalism in Egypt. In 1951, Nahas Pasha, the leader of the recently elected nationalist Wafd Party, revoked the Anglo-Egyptian Treaty of 1936, thus meaning that British troops would have to leave the country by 1955. Attacks on the British garrison soon took place and following negotiations it was agreed that, after vacating Egypt, British troops would be permitted to return if the Suez Canal was threatened by an outside power.

In October and November 1951, RAF Transport Command undertook a round-the-clock operation to fly 3,500 British reinforcements into the Canal Zone to protect the British interests up to 1955. Some 3,000 officers and men of the 19th Infantry Brigade were flown out in Hastings aircraft. When the increasing threat to life and property became untenable, the repatriation of RAF families was organised. Transport Command brought home 586 families from the Canal Zone in sixty-two round trips.

Meanwhile, on 26 September in Korea, the biggest air battle of the Korean campaign was fought over the Yalu River; seventy-seven Allied jet fighters (including Meteors flown by the RAAF pilots) and about 120 Russian fighters were involved in the conflict. In Tokyo, Air Marshal Jones, the Australian Chief of Air Staff, admitted that both the Russian MiG-15 and the American F-86 Sabre were faster than the Meteor F.8. Before the end of the year, volunteers were called for from among the RAF fighter pilots for attachment to the USAF and RAAF squadrons in Korea, for the purpose of gaining modern operational experience. The response far exceeded the requirement.

▲ Families of British servicemen wait to be evacuated from the RAF base at Ismailia following a series of violent attacks against British bases in the Canal Zone. These attacks occurred after the Egyptian Government's decision to terminate the 1936 Anglo-Egyptian Treaty on 16 October 1951. *(Crown Copyright/Air Historical Branch image CMP-217)*

▼ A night patrol mounted by members of 3 RAF Police Wing based at Ismailia, Egypt, stops in Arashiya, the suburb adjoining the British base, 26 October 1951. Security in the Canal Zone was increased earlier in the month following the newly elected Egyptian government's decision to terminate the 1936 Anglo-Egyptian Treaty, which led to a wave of anti-British protests. *(Crown Copyright/Air Historical Branch image CMP-230)*

Groundcrew of 213 Squadron preparing a de Havilland Vampire FB.5 for a reconnaissance sortie from Deversoir, Egypt, in late October 1951. *(Crown Copyright/Air Historical Branch image CMP-231)*

Gloster Meteor T.7, WF855, being prepared at an RAF airfield in Egypt for a reconnaissance sortie over the Canal Zone in November 1951. Delivered new to 213 Squadron at Deversoir, WF855 later served with 8 Squadron at Khormaksar in Aden. The aircraft was struck off charge in September 1954. *(Crown Copyright/Air Historical Branch image CMP-249)*

Following the decision by Egypt to terminate the 1936 Anglo-Egyptian Treaty in October 1951, RAF Transport Command undertook a round-the-clock operation to fly 3,500 British reinforcements into the Canal Zone. Troops of the 16th Parachute Brigade – the first to arrive in Egypt – are seen here embarking on a Handley Page Hastings C.1, TG562/DW of the Lyneham Wing, at Nicosia, Cyprus, on 1 November 1951. *(Crown Copyright/Air Historical Branch image CMP-221)*

Vampire FB.5 aircraft of 249 Squadron at Deversoir, Egypt, on 28 December 1951. At this time, tensions across the Canal Zone were high following a series of anti-British protests and the squadron, along with others in the region, were prepared to carry out pre-emptive strikes against Egyptian Air Force bases and support the British Army in an advance on Cairo in the event that the situation deteriorated further. *(Crown Copyright/Air Historical Branch image CMP-426)*

Λ An airman fitting one of the two nose-mounted F24 aerial cameras into the nose of a Gloster Meteor FR.9. This version of the
Meteor was first flown in May 1950 and was primarily used by squadrons based in the Middle East, No 208 being the first to
receive the type at Fayid, Egypt, in June 1951. *(Crown Copyright/Air Historical Branch image PRB-1-3597)*

Expediting the rearmament programme

On 29 January 1951, Prime Minister Clement Attlee
made a statement in the House of Commons. It was
intended, he said, to expedite the British rearmament
programme and call up reservists for training. World
war was not, he emphasised, inevitable, but peace
could only be ensured if the defences of the free world
were made sufficiently strong to deter aggression. 'It is
for this purpose, and this purpose only,' he said, 'that
the Government now thinks it right to take still further
measures to increase the state of preparedness of the
Armed Forces.'

When the Korean campaign began in 1950, the RAF
immediately made arrangements to increase ten-fold
its annual intake of pilot trainees (from 300 to 3,000)
and, in addition, 500 ex-RAF navigators were asked
to volunteer for further service. Then, during 1951, the

RAF recalled some 10,000 officers and men who were
required to man the control and reporting organisation
in an emergency for a further fifteen days' training.
Similarly, officers and men of the Royal Auxiliary Air
Force (RAuxAF) fighter squadrons were called up for
three months' continuous training, in order to bring
them closer to the operational standards of regular
squadrons. In addition to the RAuxAF, around 1,000
aircrew reservists of the Regular and Volunteer Reserves
were recalled for three months' refresher training, and
reserve flying instructors were recalled for up to eighteen
months, to help with the significantly increased pilot
training demands.

The practice adopted by the RAF at the start of
fighting in Korea, of retaining regulars beyond the normal
expiry of their service, was continued throughout 1951.

⋀ A 115 Squadron Washington B.1, WF495, photographed at RAF Marham on 13 October 1951, shortly before taking the Secretary of State for Air, the Lord de L'Isle and Dudley VC, on a flight during a visit to the station. *(Crown Copyright/Air Historical Branch image PRB-1-4048)*

⋁ Bomber Command Lincolns pictured during Exercise Pinnacle in October 1951. The exercise was held across Western Europe in early October with RAF and American fighters intercepting bombers attempting to 'raid' targets such as London, Birmingham and Liverpool. *(Crown Copyright/Air Historical Branch image PRB-1-3864)*

⚠ The first of four Hastings C.4 VIP transports, WD500, poses for a publicity shot at RAF Topcliffe in December 1951. The richly appointed cabin had a combined dining and conference room which doubled up as sleeping quarters for overnight flights, rear-facing leather seats and strip lighting which could be dimmed. Despite all of this apparent luxury, the passengers may occasionally have felt some discomfort in the unpressurised cabin. *(Crown Copyright/Air Historical Branch image PRB-1-3973)*

Avro Shackleton MR.1 comes into service

The value of the four-engined landplane as a long-range maritime reconnaissance aircraft was proved during the Second World War by Coastal Command's Liberators and Fortresses. For the post-war RAF, a British replacement was sought for the American-designed lend-lease aircraft. The choice made was in favour of the Avro Shackleton.

The Shackleton was developed from the Lincoln III, a projected anti-submarine reconnaissance version of the bomber, retaining the Lincoln's wings and undercarriage, but introducing a shortened, redesigned fuselage and Rolls-Royce Griffon engines driving

six-blade contra-rotating propellers. The prototype Shackleton MR.1 (VW126) made its first flight on 9 March 1949. Two further prototypes were built (VW131 and VW135) before production commenced with VP254, which made its first flight on 24 October 1950. The MR.1 was characterised by a short nose with a chin radome, seventy-seven examples of which were built.

The Shackleton MR.1 first entered service in April 1951 with 120 Squadron and 236 OCU at RAF Kinloss. Shackletons replaced Lancaster MR.3s in service, which had served since the war.

⋀ De Havilland Mosquito PR34, PF676/K, of 13 Squadron and de Havilland Vampire FB.5s of 32 Squadron pictured at Shallufa, Egypt, on 6 November 1951, prior to departing on the route-proving flight to Swartkop. It was planned that the route would be a link between Egypt and South Africa for jet aircraft, while the Mosquito aircraft acted as navigation leader for the Vampires. *(Crown Copyright/Air Historical Branch image CMP-268)*

➤ Crews and Valetta C.1 transport aircraft (VX512 illustrated) of 70 Squadron at Shallufa, Egypt, on 6 November 1951. The aircraft were about to depart on a route-proving flight from Egypt to Swartkop in South Africa, which also involved Vampires from 32 Squadron and Mosquito aircraft from **13 Squadron.** *(Crown Copyright/Air Historical Branch image CMP-266)*

The Varsity T.1 enters service

Another new type to enter service with the RAF in 1951 was the Vickers Varsity T.1. It joined 201 Advanced Flying Squadron (AFS) at RAF Swinderby on 1 October, alongside the Wellington T.10 crew training aircraft it was scheduled to replace. In order to provide facilities for bomb-aiming practice, a pannier was added beneath the fuselage, the forward portion accommodating a bomb-aiming position and the rear section providing stowage for 24 × 25lb practice bombs. Full radar and wireless equipment was carried, including H2S and Rebecca.

Developed from the Viking and Valetta transport aircraft, the first Vickers Valetta T.1 aircrew trainers entered service in late 1951. Featuring a tricycle undercarriage, the Valetta T.1 was used by Flying Training Command to train new crews destined for Lincoln bombers and for the advanced instruction of navigators and bomb-aimers. This aircraft, WF330/O, was one of the first Valetta T.1 aircraft delivered to the RAF, and was photographed shortly after joining 201 Advanced Flying School at RAF Swinderby in November 1951. *(Crown Copyright/Air Historical Branch image PRB-1-3714)*

Hawker P.1067 first flight

The forerunner of the Hawker Hunter, the Hawker P.1067 prototype (WB188) made its first flight under great secrecy at Boscombe Down on 20 July 1951. It made its first public appearance at the SBAC Show at Farnborough in September, where it caught the public's eye with a spectacular display of fast and low flying. The Hunter was to become Fighter Command's standard day fighter in the second half of the 1950s, with over 1,000 aircraft in five versions equipping squadrons throughout the service.

BAFO becomes 2 TAF

On 1 September 1951, the British Air Forces of Occupation in Germany (BAFO) were placed at the disposal of the NATO Supreme Commander. A substantial expansion was started and at the same time all units were reorganised on a fully mobile basis. The wartime title of 2nd Tactical Air Force (2 TAF) was also restored. In the same month, the British Army of the Rhine (BAOR) and the 2nd Tactical Air Force operated alongside the Belgian, Dutch, Norwegian, Danish and American formations in a large-scale tactical exercise called Counter Thrust. During the exercise, Gloster Meteor FR.9s were used in the fighter-reconnaissance role, while Meteor PR.10s were used in high-altitude photo reconnaissance activities.

Gloster Meteor FR.9, VZ603/B-A, of 2 Squadron, in flight on 16 October 1951. At the time the squadron was based at Bückeburg, Germany, with 34 Wing as part of the British Air Forces of Occupation (BAFO). *(Crown Copyright/Air Historical Branch image CLP-61)*

SBAC Show highlights

Held at Farnborough from 11–16 September 1951, the SBAC Show saw the debuts of some of the aircraft that were to shape the next decade. The most important of these was the Hawker P.1067 (WB188) which would later enter production as the Hunter, providing more than 1,000 aircraft to the RAF.

Also present was the very first of the V-bombers, the Vickers Type 660 (later to be named Valiant) prototype (WB210); the largely unsuccessful Supermarine Swift prototype in the form of the Type 535 (VV119); the de Havilland Vampire T.11 (G-5-7); and a pair of Canberra prototypes – the PR.3 (VX181) and B.5 (VX185). The RAF provided a four-ship aerobatic display of Vampire FB.5s from 54 Squadron.

In September 1951, no less an authority than the air correspondent of the *New York Herald Tribune*, reported that at the SBAC display at Farnborough: 'The cold facts are that England demonstrated the finest jet fighter and jet bomber operating in the world today.' He was, of course, referring to the Hawker P.1067, powered by a Rolls-Royce Avon engine and demonstrated with shattering effect by Hawker's Chief Test Pilot, Neville Duke; and to the four-jet-engined Valiant Bomber.

Shackleton MR.1A, WB822, flies down the runway at the 1951 SBAC Show at Farnborough during its display. At the time, the aircraft was still retained by the manufacturer – Avro – and was not delivered to its first unit, 236 Operational Conversion Unit at RAF Kinloss, until December 1951. *(Crown Copyright/Air Historical Branch image PRB-1-3375)*

A WF320, the prototype Blackburn and General Aircraft Universal Freighter, on display at the 1951 SBAC Show at Farnborough, which took place from 11–16 September. Despite its bulky appearance, the aircraft impressed onlookers with its impressive take-off and landing capabilities, as well as its ability to taxi backwards on the runway. The Universal Freighter was developed into the Beverley for use by the RAF, with deliveries to Transport Command squadrons commencing in 1956. This photograph captures the two largest land-based aircraft built by British companies at the time. Even with its impressive dimensions (162ft wingspan, 38ft 9in high and capable of carrying a load of 45,000lbs), the aircraft was dwarfed by the eight-engined Bristol Brabazon airliner – the sole example of which can be seen in the background of this picture – which had a wingspan of 230ft and a length of 177ft. At the time, *Flight* magazine reported that the Universal Freighter had brought a 22ft caravan and Land Rover to the show in its hold and continued, 'That eminently practical pilot, "Tim" Wood, announced his intention of flying from Brough to Farnborough at great heights, and with the heaters off, in order that the refreshing beverages in the caravan should arrive well iced." *(Crown Copyright/Air Historical Branch image PRB-1-3377)*

V In addition to the three 'V-Bombers' ordered by the RAF – Valiant, Vulcan and Victor – a fourth design, the SA.4 Sperrin, was designed to meet the same Air Ministry Specification by Short. The least radical of all the proposals, the Sperrin featured a straight wing with four Rolls-Royce Avon engines mounted in pairs and arranged one above the other. Of the five-man crew, only the pilot had an ejection seat. Its huge, slab-sided fuselage featured a bomb bay measuring 30ft long, 10ft deep and 10ft wide. By the time of its maiden flight in August 1951, the design had lost out to the Valiant and only two airframes were completed. VX158 went on to be used as a trials aircraft for the unsuccessful Gyron engine, while the second Sperrin, VX161, was used to drop dummy concrete bombs of new designs, including the Blue Danube plutonium device. *(Crown Copyright/Air Historical Branch image PRB-1-3378)*

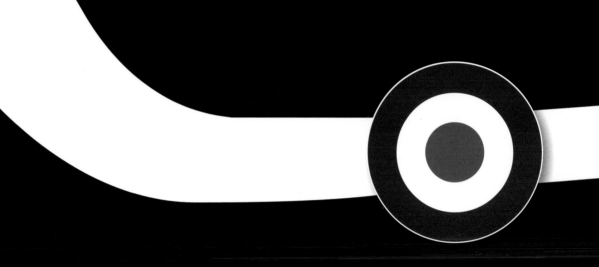

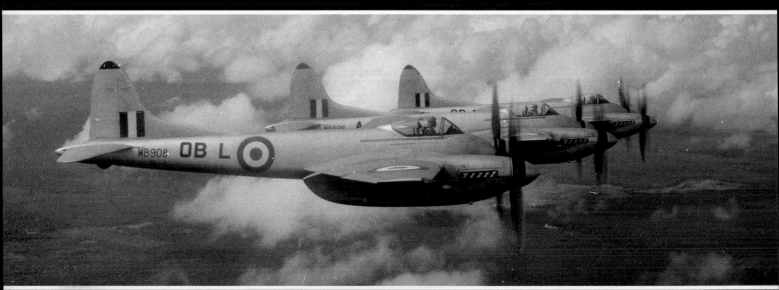

1952

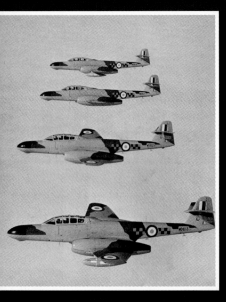

State of the nation

The accelerated defence measures put in place by the Labour Government as a result of both Cold War pressures in Europe and the conflict in Korea meant that when the Conservative Government returned to power in the autumn of 1951 – with Winston Churchill as Prime Minister and Secretary of State for Defence – they found themselves facing a likely defence expenditure of £4,700 million over the following three years, to fund a greatly expanded rearmament programme.

It had been planned that defence production would rise at the peak of the expansion programme to more than four times that of pre-Korean War levels; but the economic position had seriously deteriorated and it became necessary to adjust the defence programme so that it would take more than the originally anticipated three years to achieve. The aircraft programme in particular, which included several new production lines for jet engines, required the building up of a large labour force. Before the programme had started, around 150,000 people were employed in the UK aircraft industry but, by March 1953, this number had increased to nearer 200,000.

Building up strength was not just a question of new equipment – there was also the problem of adequate, suitably trained manpower to operate it. Regular recruiting on long-term non-commissioned engagements in 1952 proved disappointing. The three-year short-term engagement introduced by the RAF in 1950 had, however, produced good results. It involved three years in the Colours with the Regular force, followed by a period of reserve service. Short-term engagements were only genuinely fruitful if a reasonable proportion of initially short-term recruits extended their service and re-engaged, but insufficient numbers of men showed signs of doing this. It was nevertheless fair to say that the attractions of the new trade structure and the pay increases of September 1950 had resulted in

more recruits joining the RAF in the period from 1951 to 1953 than in the three preceding years. Clearly, there were challenges ahead.

Around this time, RAF flying training received significant help from the Royal Canadian Air Force (RCAF). During 1952 there were nearly 800 RAF pilots and navigators undergoing flying training in Canada. During the war, under the British Commonwealth air training scheme, Canada had trained around 131,000 aircrew and now, as a result of the RAF's expansion at the time of the Korean War, she had once again become part of

Λ Flames from the engine of de Havilland Vampire NF.10, WP252, of 25 Squadron are photographed on engine start-up as the aircraft is prepared for a night sortie from RAF West Malling on 26 January 1952. *(Crown Copyright/Air Historical Branch image T-30)*

a vast aircrew training programme with schools in Ontario, Manitoba, Alberta and British Columbia. One problem that resulted from training in the excellent visibility conditions in Canada (with the Rockies often visible from up to 100 miles away), was that on return to the smoke and mist of the British Isles and the multiplicity of landmarks in a densely populated island, acclimatisation courses proved necessary to help Canadian-trained pilots and navigators adjust to the significantly different weather conditions in general, and to the poor visibility in particular.

In February 1952, there came the end of an era when a composite detachment of 350 officers and men, drawn from all RAF Commands at home, the RAF Regiment and the Royal Auxiliary Air Force, led the funeral procession of His Majesty King George VI from Westminster Hall (where he had been lying in state) to Paddington station. His funeral took place at St George's Chapel, Windsor Castle, on 15 February. He was succeeded by his daughter Elizabeth.

Overseas conflicts

Throughout 1952, Britain was still involved with emergencies in both Malaya and Korea. Throughout the Malayan conflict, an extensive campaign of psychological warfare was mounted. The objective was to encourage the surrender of the communist terrorists (CT) through disaffection, especially at junior ranks, and to win the hearts and minds of the uncommitted population. In the first instance, the leaflet-drops were of a strategic nature, advising the population of the emergency, but the emphasis quickly turned to tactical drops, often in association with operations, and the majority called for the surrender of the CT, often naming individuals. Surrendered CTs were often used to draft the leaflets. As an indication of the efforts involved, during the peak month for leaflet-dropping (October 1953) 19,536,000 leaflets were dispersed in fifty-one sorties, many in association with Operation Bison 1. In November 1952, a new twist was added to the arsenal of psychological warfare when loud-hailer aircraft were used for 'skyshouting' during the operation.

The use of broadcasts from aircraft was first tested in October 1952, using a borrowed US Army C-47. Following further trials and experiments with an Auster, the RAF fitted the equipment to a pair of Valetta aircraft. The Valetta suffered from excessive engine noise, limiting the range of broadcasts, so the RAF turned to the Dakota, three of which were fitted with a battery of speakers. Whereas the Valetta had to fly at 1,500ft to be heard over a 1,500-yard range, the Dakota could fly at 2,500ft and be heard over a range of 2,500 yards.

For many years before the Second World War there was dissension in Kenya on the part of the Kikuyu tribe in the Central Province to the north of Nairobi. It was felt that Europeans had deprived them of their lands. After the war the Kenyan African Union (KAU) was formed and from it sprang an extremist group, the Mau Mau, which also called itself the Kenyan Land Freedom Party. As the population grew, pressure on the land was such that indigenous peoples found themselves working on increasingly less advantageous terms than European

Λ A de Havilland Hornet F.3, WB870/5R-M, of 33 Squadron is rearmed and refuelled at an airfield in Malaya after a mission against communist forces in early 1952. No 33 Squadron had taken on the Hornet F.3 in May 1951 and operated the type until the squadron was disbanded in March 1955. *(Crown Copyright/Air Historical Branch image CFP-511a)*

farmers. In 1948 and 1949 there was discontent among the labour force and the local RAF Communications Flight was involved in leaflet-dropping.

Throughout 1952 there were isolated attacks on white farmers. By no means did all Kikuyu people support the Mau Mau, and it was the murder on 9 October 1952 of Chief Waruhiu, a close British ally, that led to a state of emergency being declared on 21 October 1952. That day, troops from the 1st Battalion, Lancashire Fusiliers, were flown into Nairobi on Hastings transport aircraft from 511 Squadron, joining four battalions of the King's African Rifles and the Kenyan Regiment already in the country.

At the time, RAF strength in Kenya amounted to six aircraft in a Communications Flight based at Eastleigh. These included two Dakota aircraft left by 82 Squadron when it returned to the UK in October following a survey. As the Rhodesian Air Training Group (RATG) was being disbanded, a number of its Harvard IIB aircraft were formed into 1340 Flight at Thornhill before moving

to Eastleigh on 23 March 1953. From here it began bombing operations against the Mau Mau using small fragmentation bombs. The conflict in Kenya was to continue right through to 1956.

Britain had long maintained close links with Oman through a succession of treaties to protect her oil interests and sea routes. For many years Saudi Arabia had contested the border at the key crossroads of Buraimi Oasis, but when the area was suspected to have potential oil reserves, a small Saudi party of about eighty settled in the nearby village of Hamasa on 31 August 1952. The British Government protested and from 15 September a small force of Trucial Oman Levies (TOL) was dispatched to the village and three Vampire FB.5 aircraft of 6 Squadron, supported by a Valetta, were flown to Sharjah from Habbaniyah. After demonstrations and leaflet-drops, talks began and the aircraft returned to Iraq in October. Talks continued but dragged on without a clear resolution and the RAF's involvement in Oman would continue on until 1959.

Another view of 33 Squadron de Havilland Hornet F.3s at a rain-soaked Butterworth airfield in Malaya, early 1952.
(Crown Copyright/Air Historical Branch image CFP-539)

▲ Armourers load a bomb under the wing of a de Havilland Hornet F.3, WB875, of 33 Squadron at Butterworth, Malaya, in preparation for an airstrike on a communist target in the country in 1952. *(Crown Copyright/Air Historical Branch image CFP-540)*

▼ Bristol Brigand B.1, RH776/K, of 84 Squadron based at Tengah, Singapore, returning from an anti-terrorist attack in the Malayan jungle in mid-1952. *(Crown Copyright/Air Historical Branch image CFP-595)*

▲ Another 84 Squadron Bristol Brigand B.1, being prepared for an anti-terrorist rocket attack in the Malayan jungle in mid-1952. *(Crown Copyright/Air Historical Branch image CFP-601)*

▼ Three de Havilland Hornet F.3s – WB898/OB-A, WB908/OB-L and WB911/OB-B – of 45 Squadron on patrol over the Malayan jungle in mid-1952. This version of the single-seat Hornet was optimised for ground-attack duties in the Far East using rocket projectiles and had a range of 3,000 miles. *(Crown Copyright/Air Historical Branch image CFP-608)*

➤ Airmen check the external mounting points under the forward fuselage of a Handley Page Hastings temporarily flying with a Parachute Training Unit in Egypt. The aircraft has been loaded with two jeeps which were to be dropped by parachute during a training exercise with Army troops on 4 February 1952. A line of unidentified late model Spitfires can be seen in the distance under the wing of the Hastings. *(Crown Copyright/Air Historical Branch image CMP-500)*

Ｖ Paratroops of the 16th Independent Parachute Group jumping from Handley Page Hastings C1, TG580/A, during a demonstration drop in the Canal Zone on 4 February 1952. The aircraft is also carrying a Land Rover and 75mm howitzer in special external carriers under the forward fuselage. The aircraft is from the Station Flight at RAF Abingdon. The Great Bitter Lake can be seen in the distance. *(Crown Copyright/Air Historical Branch image CMP-498)*

⋀ With the Ataqa Hills seen in the hazy distance, groundcrew service a Vampire FB.9 – WL580 of 6 Squadron – shortly after its arrival at Fayid, Egypt, from Abu Sueir on 8 April 1952. *(Crown Copyright/Air Historical Branch image CMP-524)*

◤ Engine fitters working on one of the propellers of an Avro York after landing at Fayid, Egypt, on 8 April 1952. Some sources indicate that the serial WW502 was in a batch 'used temporarily for civilian Avro York aircraft flying into the Canal Zone under treaty'. The civilian registration of the aircraft is known to be G-AHFH. *(Crown Copyright/Air Historical Branch image CMP-525)*

Seven Gloster Meteor FR.9 aircraft of 208 Squadron, based at Abu Sueir, Egypt, photographed in formation during a flight over the Canal Zone on 9 May 1952. The aircraft shown are VW368/S, VZ578/R, VZ594/C, VZ592/B, VW370/A, VW363/O and VZ583/N. *(Crown Copyright/Air Historical Branch image CMP-515)*

Gloster Meteor FR.9 aircraft of 208 Squadron based at Abu Sueir, Egypt, photographed while looping in formation during a training sortie over the Canal Zone on 9 May 1952. *(Crown Copyright/Air Historical Branch image CMP-518)*

The personal Vickers Valetta C.2 used by General Sir Brian Robertson, Commander-in-Chief Middle East Land Forces, being serviced at Fayid, Egypt, on 8 April 1952. *(Crown Copyright/Air Historical Branch image CMP-526)*

Four Shackleton MR.1A aircraft of 220 Squadron flying over coconut plantations in the vicinity of the old Dutch port of Galle in Southern Ceylon during a ten-day visit to the island in February 1952. *(Crown Copyright/Air Historical Branch image CFP-559)*

▲ Four de Havilland Vampire FB.5s of 93 Squadron, part of 112 Wing based at Jever, Germany, photographed in flight on 4 March 1952. The aircraft are WA319/T-D, WA191/T-G, VZ341/T-S and WA133/T-B. *(Crown Copyright/Air Historical Branch CLP-77)*

▼ The pilot of Vampire FB.5, WA319/T-D, from 93 Squadron based at Celle, fires a salvo of unguided rocket projectiles at a target on an air weapons range in Germany, 4 March 1952. *(Crown Copyright/Air Historical Branch CLP-76)*

Training in Rhodesia

In the immediate post-war period, the Air Ministry recognised the benefits of the excellent flying conditions offered by Rhodesia and signed an agreement to revive the flying training programme in the African country. Two stations were opened at Heany and Thornhill where Nos 4 (operating the Chipmunk) and 5 (operating the Harvard) Flying Training Schools were respectively based.

⋁ In the immediate post-war period, the Air Ministry, recognising the benefits of the excellent flying conditions offered by Rhodesia, signed an agreement to revive the flying training programme at two stations. Nos 4 and 5 Flying Training Schools, based at Heany and Thornhill respectively, operated the Chipmunk and Harvard. This was the scene at Thornhill in May 1952 where a line of Chipmunks waited for their next students. *(Crown Copyright/Air Historical Branch image CMP-533)*

⋁ Five Sunderland GR.5s from 201 Squadron are seen here anchored in a bay on Malta during a visit to the island from their base at Pembroke Dock, June 1952. *(Crown Copyright/Air Historical Branch image CMP-573)*

➤ Six Vampire FB.5s of 613 Squadron Royal Auxiliary Air Force flying over Malta during the squadron's summer training camp to Luqa in August 1952. *(Crown Copyright/Air Historical Branch image CMP-599)*

🗸 The first RAF squadron to receive the Canberra B.2 was No 101, based at RAF Binbrook, which replaced its Lincoln bombers (two of which can be seen in the distance) from mid-1951 onwards. Nine of the new Canberra aircraft are seen here lined up at the Lincolnshire base on 10 January 1952. *(Crown Copyright/Air Historical Branch image PRB-1-4141)*

Neptunes fill a gap

On 27 January 1952 the first of fifty-two Lockheed Neptune MR.1 maritime reconnaissance aircraft (WX493 and WX494) entered RAF service. They were initially introduced with 217 Squadron at St Eval, although this unit moved to RAF Kinloss in April 1952. Similar to the US Navy's Lockheed P2V-5, it acted as a stop-gap with Coastal Command until the Avro Shackleton entered service. The Neptune MR.1 equipped four UK-based squadrons. With a crew of ten (two pilots, two navigators, five air signallers and an engineer) and an 8,000lb weapon load, the long-range Neptunes were returned to the US in 1957 after being replaced in service with Avro Shackleton aircraft.

˅ The first Lockheed Neptune MR.1 supplied to the RAF under the Mutual Defence Aid Programme, WX493, pictured at St Eval, Cornwall, on 13 January 1952. Fifty-two former US Navy aircraft were operated by Coastal Command as a stop-gap measure until 1957, when they were replaced by the Avro Shackleton. Four Neptunes were modified for service with Fighter Command for airborne early warning duties between 1952 and 1956 with 1453 Flight based at RAF Topcliffe. *(Crown Copyright/Air Historical Branch image PRB-1-4153)*

Aircraft retired from RAF service and stored at 20 Maintenance Unit at RAF Aston Down, Gloucestershire, photographed on 13 February 1952. Types visible include Tempest F.2s, Lincolns, Lancasters and Hastings. Each of the aircraft has been covered in a protective coating to preserve the airframe should it be required to see further service with another operator. *(Crown Copyright/Air Historical Branch image PRB-1-4278)*

Another view of aircraft in storage at 20 Maintenance Unit, RAF Aston Down, 13 February 1952. The aircraft closest to the camera is Lincoln B.2, RE406. Despite never flying operationally with the RAF after it was completed in January 1946, the aircraft underwent a series of modifications in 1948 to B2/4A standard before being delivered to Aston Down. Declared as 'non-effective' in June 1954, it was subsequently sold for scrap in July 1955. *(Crown Copyright/Air Historical Branch image PRB-1-4279)*

↖ Three Meteor T.7s of the Central Flying School's (CFS) Meteorites display team emulate a formation similar to that flown by a pre-war CFS Avro Tutor team in 1933. Squadron Leader George Brabyn flies his Meteor T.7, WF852, inverted, with wingmen Flight Lieutenants James and Price (WH241/N-D and WA691/Y-D) in tight formation during a photographic sortie from RAF Little Rissington on 28 March 1952. This was done for the school's 1952 Christmas card. Attempting it with the jet-powered Meteor took great skill as the lead aircraft could only remain inverted for fifteen seconds before the pilot would have to roll upright owing to a lack of fuel flow to the engine while in the inverted position. *(Crown Copyright/Air Historical Branch image PRB-1-4360)*

∨ Four Meteor NF.11s (WD615, WD625, WD617 and WD618) from 85 Squadron based at RAF West Malling, photographed on **19 May 1952.** *(Crown Copyright/ Air Historical Branch image PRB-1-4580)*

↖ An unusual mixed formation flown by the Central Flying School on 12 May 1952 to mark the school's fortieth anniversary demonstrates the wide variety of aircraft operated by the CFS at the time. Taking part in the formation are: Avro Anson C.19, TX191/I-G; Supermarine Spitfire LF.XVIe, SL721/JMR; Gloster Meteor T.7, WH245/ O-M; North American Harvard IIB, FT213/N-L; and de Havilland Vampire FB.5, WE830/I-H. The Spitfire was the personal aircraft of Air Chief Marshal Sir James Robb, the Air Officer Commander-in-Chief of Fighter Command, until his retirement in 1951. It was then used by the CFS until 1954 and retained the personal code 'JMR'. The Vampire crashed barely a week after this photo was taken when it stalled on approach while attempting to land at RAF Little Rissington on 21 May. *(Crown Copyright/Air Historical Branch image PRB-1-4555)*

First British-designed helicopter enters service

The Bristol Sycamore was the first British-designed helicopter to enter service with the RAF. It was developed from the original Bristol Type 171 Mk.1, the first prototype of which (VL958) had made its first flight on 24 July 1947. The prototype had been powered by a Pratt & Whitney R-985 Wasp Junior engine of 450hp, but production aircraft utilised the 550hp Alvis Leonides engine.

The first version developed was the HR.12 search and rescue and anti-submarine reconnaissance version for the RAF. The first Sycamore HR.12 (WV781) was delivered to St Mawgan for trials with the Coastal Command Development Unit on 19 February 1952. It was subsequently joined by three other airframes (WV782, 783 and 784).

Bristol Sycamore HR.12, WV781/FZ, of the Air-Sea Warfare Development Unit, photographed at RAF St Mawgan on 24 May 1952, shortly after the helicopter had been delivered on 19 February. The Sycamore was the first British-designed helicopter to enter service with the RAF at home or overseas. *(Crown Copyright/Air Historical Branch image PRB-1-4639)*

Sikorsky S-55, XA842, pictured at Fort Southwick, near Portsmouth, on 24 June 1952, having carried senior officers to view Exercise Castanets, a large-scale NATO air-sea exercise held in British waters in the preceding two weeks. XA842 was a Sikorsky-built S-55 registered as G-AMHK to Westland as a company demonstrator. It was subsequently given the military serial of WW339 for trials with the Air Ministry in early 1952 before receiving its current identity following a series of modifications. It was later sold in Norway as LN-ORK. *(Crown Copyright/Air Historical Branch image PRB-1-4789)*

⋀ 220 Squadron Avro Shackleton MR.1A, WB831, photographed at RAF St Mawgan on 24 May 1952. The Shackleton was developed from a proposed anti-submarine reconnaissance version of the Avro Lincoln – the Mark III. It retained the Lincoln's wing, tail and undercarriage, married to a shorter, redesigned fuselage. The early Shackletons had a short nose and chin radome, but from the Mark 2 onwards, this was lengthened and streamlined. WB831 was one of seventeen Shackleton MR.1s later converted to a T.4 training aircraft with additional radar positions for instructors and students. *(Crown Copyright/Air Historical Branch image PRB-1-4640)*

⋁ Avro Lancaster GR.3, SW324, of 210 Squadron photographed at RAF St Mawgan on 24 May 1952. After the end of the Second World War, Coastal Command Liberators were returned to the USA and the Lancaster became the RAF's principal land-based maritime reconnaissance aircraft until the arrival of the former US Navy Neptune aircraft under the MDAP Programme (see page 109) and the Avro Shackleton MR.1A in the early 1950s (see above). The bomb bays of these aircraft were modified to carry an airborne lifeboat (pictured). The very last Lancaster in RAF service was a Coastal Command example which was finally retired on 15 October 1956. *(Crown Copyright/Air Historical Branch image PRB-1-4641)*

British North Greenland Expedition

An official operation order was received stating that five Sunderland GR.5 aircraft would proceed via Reykjavik (Iceland) to Young Sound (latitude 74° north) and would support the British North Greenland Expedition by transporting 150 tons of stores, dogs and passengers to Britannia Lake (at latitude 77° north). The detachment of forty aircrew and twenty groundcrew was placed under the command of Squadron Leader J.S. Higgins DFC, AFC, Officer Commanding 230 Squadron.

On 21 July 1952, the first Sunderland – commanded by Squadron Leader Higgins – left Pembroke Dock, landing at Reykjavik later that afternoon. Several attempts were made to survey the ice en route to Young Sound, with a view to aiding the MV *Tottan* which was carrying the expedition party and stores to Young Sound. Because of the adverse weather conditions, the survey was not completed until 28 July; and then only

from an altitude of 8,000ft as the weather conditions below were still poor.

By 30 July a signal was received from the MV *Tottan* at Young Sound that the landing area was clear of ice and the weather fine. The first aircraft (SZ581/Y) landed at Young Sound at around 17.15 and the RAF ensign flew over Young Sound for the very first time. Another Sunderland (RN270/O) landed at around 20.15, having suffered slight engine problems.

On 3 August, Higgins set out for Britannia Lake but, on arrival over the lake, it was found to be almost entirely frozen over and impossible to alight onto. Later, on 5 August, Higgins made an attempt to land on the water in an unladen aircraft (RN299/P) to test the approach. Finding the lake almost completely free of ice, he touched down at 10.15 and the aircraft became the first ever to alight on Britannia Lake. Once suitable

◄ **Short Sunderland GR.5s of 230 Squadron photographed at Pembroke Dock, Wales, on 20 July 1952. On the following day the first of five Sunderland aircraft took off for Reykjavik, Iceland, in readiness to commence a month-long airlift to the British North Greenland Expedition based at Young Sound in the Arctic Circle.** *(Crown Copyright/Air Historical Branch image PRB-1-4969)*

➤ **Short Sunderland GR.5 of 230 Squadron resupplying the British North Greenland Expedition while based at Young Sound in August 1952. The mountains of Clavering Island provide the dramatic backdrop across Britannia Lake.** *(Crown Copyright/Air Historical Branch image PRB-1-5172)*

anchorage had been located, the crew rowed ashore and selected an area in which to set up camp.

Fog prevented the airlift commencing the following morning and it was not until 7 August that the airlift could actually take place.

On 13 August one of the Sunderland aircraft suffered a major engine problem twenty minutes after taking off from Britannia Lake and only just cleared the 7,000ft-high ice-capped mountains in its path.

Despite further bad weather, including very low temperatures, strong winds, fog and snow, the airlift was duly completed by 19 August. The last three aircraft left Young Sound for Reykjavik on 22 August and all aircraft arrived back at Pembroke Dock the following day.

Venom fighter-bomber enters service

The prototype Venom (VV612) made its first flight on 2 September 1949. Powered by the Ghost engine, the aircraft offered a significant performance improvement on the Goblin-powered Vampire. In August 1952, the first Venom FB.1 aircraft were delivered to No 11

Squadron at Wunstorf in Germany, part of the 2nd Allied Tactical Air Force. A total of 370 Venom FB.1s were eventually built.

SBAC Show highlights

The SBAC Show of 1952, held at Farnborough from 1–7 September, was the most popular of all time, with over 300,000 people attending the event. Sadly, the 1952 show will always be associated with disaster – the DH.110 broke up in the air during a low run, killing pilot John Derry and navigator Tony Richards. Twenty-nine spectators were also killed, and a further sixty were injured.

The star of the show was undoubtedly VX770, the Avro 698 (Vulcan) prototype which appeared at Farnborough just three days after making its maiden flight. It flew in company with the Avro 707 research aircraft. Other debutants included the Gloster Javelin, Bristol Britannia and Princess flying boat, the latter another white elephant in the Brabazon mould!

The shape of things to come: prototypes of two of the RAF's proposed V-Bombers pictured at the 1952 SBAC Show at Farnborough. Roly Falk, Chief Test Pilot with Avro, banks the first Type 698, VX770, to display the aircraft's distinctive delta shape while the second, the Vickers Valiant WB215, waits for clearance to commence its display. *(Crown Copyright/Air Historical Branch image PRB-1-5217)*

The second Handley Page Marathon T.11, XA250, commencing its display at the SBAC Show at Farnborough in September 1952. Twenty-eight Marathons were supplied to the RAF for use as trainers at 2 Air Navigation School based at RAF Thorney Island from April 1954. The RAF, which had the aircraft virtually forced upon it by the Ministry of Supply, found it difficult to keep them serviceable and the type was eventually retired in 1958. *(Crown Copyright/Air Historical Branch image PRB-1-5213a)*

Five Canberra B.2 aircraft from 101 Squadron, based at RAF Binbrook, photographed in formation on 10 September 1952. The aircraft wear a variety of colour schemes; two are painted in camouflaged upper fuselage and wings while the remainder carry the blue/black colours originally applied to the early Canberra aircraft. *(Crown Copyright/Air Historical Branch image PRB-1-5260)*

➢ The prototype Avro 698 Vulcan, VX770, banks away from the camera to display the delta plan form of the aircraft in October 1952. VX770 had made its first flight on 3 August 1952. *(Crown Copyright/Air Historical Branch image PRB-1-5523)*

≺ A Gloster Javelin FAW.1 displays the fighter's delta-wing shape to spectacular effect during a photoshoot in October 1952. *(Crown Copyright/Air Historical Branch image PRB-1-5543)*

Shackleton MR.2

The prototype Shackleton MR.2 (WB833 – converted from an earlier MR.1A) made its first flight on 17 June 1952 and was exhibited at the SBAC Show at Farnborough in September. Seventy MR.2 aircraft were delivered to the RAF, the first squadron being No 42 at St Eval in January 1953. The MR.2 featured a redesigned and lengthened nose and a transparent tail cone to aid visual searches. The underbelly 'dustbin' contained the search radar.

➤ A dramatic air-to-air study of the first full prototype Shackleton MR.2, WB833, photographed in flight during October 1952. The Mark 2 featured a redesigned and lengthened nose and a transparent tail cone to aid visual searches. The underbelly 'dustbin' contained the search radar (which is shown here extended), while the doors of the capacious bomb bay are clearly visible. *(Crown Copyright/Air Historical Branch image PRB-1-5544)*

◄ The prototype Hawker Hunter, WB188, photographed in October 1952. *(Crown Copyright/Air Historical Branch image PRB-1-5547)*

Hastings crash in Greenland

On 16 September, Hastings C.2, WD492, from RAF Topcliffe, crashed while carrying out a resupply drop to the British North Greenland Expedition. After initially carrying out a parachute drop from 400ft without incident, the pilot took the aircraft down to 50ft to drop the remainder of the supplies. During the drop, the aircraft became enveloped in a 'whiteout' and crashed onto the ice, injuring three of the twelve-man crew. While waiting to be rescued, the crew remained with the aircraft, draping parachutes inside the fuselage and placing sacking on the floor to provide some measure of insulation against the -17°C temperature. Members of the expedition travelled from their base a mile away to set up a small camp next to the aircraft until a rescue could be attempted. Spirits were kept high inside the Hastings – even to the extent that a party was held on the fourth night! Eventually, a Grumman Albatross amphibious aircraft from the US Air Force landed to fly the three injured men out. The final nine were airlifted out in a US Air Force Dakota to Thule Air Force Base after spending nine nights on the ice-cap.

V On 16 September, Hastings C.2, WD492, from RAF Topcliffe, crashed while carrying out a resupply drop to the British North Greenland Expedition. After initially carrying out a parachute drop from 400ft without incident, the pilot took the aircraft down to 50ft to drop the remainder of the supplies. During the drop, the aircraft became enveloped in a 'whiteout' and crashed onto the ice, injuring three of the twelve-man crew Eventually, a Grumman Albatross amphibious aircraft from the US Air Force landed to fly the three injured men out, while the final nine were airlifted out in a US Air Force Dakota after spending nine nights on the ice-cap. *(Crown Copyright/Air Historical Branch image PRB-1-5368)*

⋀ The first production-standard Supermarine Swift F.1, WK194, photographed in October 1952 during a pre-delivery test flight. At the time of the photograph, the aircraft had not been painted, and displays the various coloured panels that made up the **aircraft.** *(Crown Copyright/Air Historical Branch image PRB-1-5551)*

➤ Four Canberra B.2 aircraft of 12 Squadron (WD987, WD990, WD993 and WD996) lined up at Pistarini airport, Buenos Aires, Argentina, during a six-week goodwill visit by the squadron to South America between October and December 1952. *(Crown Copyright/ Air Historical Branch image PRB-1-5685)*

The second prototype Percival P.56 Provost, WE530, photographed in flight during late 1952. The Provost was the last piston-engined basic training aircraft ordered by the RAF and its introduction with Flying Training Schools from 1953 onwards allowed the RAF to introduce a new flying training syllabus with pilots receiving instruction on the Provost before proceeding to the Vampire jet-powered advanced trainer. *(Crown Copyright/Air Historical Branch image PRB-1-5789)*

First atomic weapons tests

On 3 October 1952 the RAF participated in the first British atomic weapon tests in the Monte Bello Islands in the Indian Ocean off Western Australia. Two nuclear capsules were loaded aboard the frigate HMS *Plym* in the Thames Estuary. When fitted with its fissile material, the warhead would weight 3 tons, about two-thirds the weight of the Blue Danube bomb. Each piece of radioactive material was transported in specially designed containers which had to be crashproof, waterproof, fireproof and, most importantly, would float. All were carried aboard Hastings and Sunderland aircraft; the Hastings routing from Lyneham through Malta, Sharjah, Negombo and Seletar in Singapore. The materials were transferred to a Sunderland which was riding at anchor in the Strait of Malacca. Airborne almost immediately, the Sunderland flew uneventfully to land on the sea at Monte Bello.

The device was loaded onto HMS *Plym* and after rehearsals, the main task force was moved some distance from Monte Bello, leaving just a few aboard the ship to prepare the explosion that would destroy the vessel. After leaving the vessel by ship, they moved a safe distance away.

At 09.30 local time, the device was detonated by cable from the island of Trimouille, sending up an expanding fireball and associated mushroom cloud to about 10,000ft. Nothing remained of HMS *Plym*.

First flight of the Handley Page Victor

The prototype Handley Page HP.80, WB771 (yet to be named Victor), made its maiden flight on 24 December 1952. The last of the three 'V-Bomber' designs to enter service, the Victor's futuristic look featured a crescent-shaped wing and was described at the time by Sir Frederick Handley Page in an issue of *Flight* magazine as 'the climax of an inspired concept, brilliant research and years of very hard work.'

1953

Following her accession to the throne on
6 February 1952, Her Majesty Queen Elizabeth II's
Coronation was held at Westminster Abbey on
2 June 1953. For the Royal Air Force, 1953
would be dominated by the planned Coronation
Review of the Royal Air Force by HM the Queen
at RAF Odiham on Wednesday 15 July. The
flypast, under the control of Air Vice-Marshal the
Earl of Bandon, was to include 640 aircraft, of
which 440 would be jet-powered.

On 2 January 1953, the first batch of Canadair-
built Sabre F.1 and F.4 aircraft for the RAF were
handed over during a ceremony at RAF Abingdon
by Mr Norman Robertson, the Canadian High
Commissioner, to the Secretary of State for Air,
the Lord de L'Isle and Dudley VC. The aircraft
had been ferried from Canada to the UK by pilots
of the Transport Command Overseas Ferry Unit
(later 147 Squadron) in an operation named
Becher's Brook which lasted from 8 December
1952 to 19 December 1953. The Sabre was the
RAF's first swept-wing fighter and was acquired
as a stop-gap measure to equip the RAF with
a fighter in the 700mph class until the Hawker
Hunter could enter service; which it eventually did
in the spring of 1955.

In total 430 Sabre F.1 and F.4 aircraft were
acquired under the Mutual Defence Aid
Programme. The first fighter squadrons to equip
with them were Nos 3 (in May 1953), 67 (May
1953) and 71 (October 1953), which together
formed the Wildenrath Wing in the 2nd Tactical
Air Force (2 TAF). In December 1953, Sabres
were delivered to 66 Squadron at RAF Linton-on-
Ouse, to become the first swept-wing fighters in
Fighter Command.

The Coronation Review of the Royal Air Force by HM Queen Elizabeth II at RAF Odiham, 15 July 1953. The culmination of seven months' careful planning can be seen in this aerial view of the immaculately parked aircraft and their crews as they wait in the afternoon sun for HM the Queen to inspect them. *(Crown Copyright/Air Historical Branch AHB-UNK-Coronation Review-Colour-12)*

The Queen's Review

The Coronation Review of the Royal Air Force by HM the Queen was held at RAF Odiham. *Flight* magazine of 24 July 1953 described the event perfectly.

'Wednesday, July 15th, was a Royal day for the RAF; and it was with fittingly royal excellence that the Service presented itself for review by its Sovereign on that day. On the ground and in the air, the men and machines that together form the modern RAF were arrayed – inspiring in appearance and precise in formation. Their contribution to the tradition of this country's youngest Service was impressive, perfectly disciplined, and indeed unforgettable.'

The event was an enormous test of the RAF's planning and culminated in more than 300 aircraft available for inspection by HM the Queen on the ground at Odiham, with a flypast led by one helicopter and containing 640 aircraft, of which 440 were jet-powered. The flypast ran with absolute precision.

The Queen's colours were escorted on to the central parade shortly before Her Majesty's arrival, with the long rows of precisely parked shining aircraft on either side. Behind these were rows of training aircraft, many carrying yellow bands as were typical of the day. Even the weather was relatively kind for the event, although the forecasted 'showers with bright intervals' were experienced. Her Majesty had chosen to wear sky blue on the day, which co-ordinated well with the dark blue uniforms on parade. The Duke of Edinburgh wore the uniform of a marshal of the RAF, with the royal blue sash of the Order of the Garter.

The morning was taken up by the marching past the dais of the various Command contingents with Bomber Command leading. As the ceremonial parade came to an end and the royal party left for lunch, white trails in sweeping curves were traced in the blue sky above by a trio of aircraft flying at 10,000ft. As a fourth aircraft swept in to add a final stroke, the letters 'E.R.' were seen to be formed, gradually widening and moving in the upper air winds. The sky writing had been performed by four Venoms of the Central Fighter Establishment.

The royal party returned to the airfield at 14.30 when Her Majesty toured the lines of parked aircraft and their crews in an open car, stopping to chat with many. Once along the final line of aircraft, the swept-wing Sabres and de Havilland Venoms of the 2nd TAF, the party

returned to the dais ready for the main event – the flypast of 640 aircraft. A specially constructed ground glass screen, showing a map of the United Kingdom and the routes taken by the participating aircraft, was used to explain the complex timing arrangements to Her Majesty.

The first pass was made by a Sycamore towing a large RAF ensign in the stiff breeze, and it passed the royal dais exactly to the scheduled second. Right behind were the Chipmunks, some rocking in the strong winds, but maintaining good formation. Prentices droned in at 600ft, followed by a neat formation of Harvards. And so the flypast continued until all 640 aircraft and helicopters had passed the royal dais; all individual aircraft and formations exactly on time. The final pass was carried out by Mike Lithgow in the blue Supermarine Swift which left in a reheat roar to bring proceedings to a close.

As the complete ground parade – and the spectators – gave three resounding cheers for Her Majesty, the sky-writing Venoms returned above to write a fitting signal for the royal occasion, 'Vivat' – simply meaning 'long live'.

▼ The lucky guests attending the review at Odiham and travelling by coach to the event were issued with commemorative tickets similar to this one for the return journey from London. *(Crown Copyright/Air Historical Branch AHB-UNK-Coronation Review-Ticket)*

CORONATION   REVIEW

OF   THE

ROYAL AIR FORCE

ODIHAM   15TH JULY 1953

COACH TICKET

LONDON (HORSE GUARDS PARADE) TO ODIHAM

AND RETURN

OUTWARD JOURNEY :   DEPART **0745-0815** HRS
RETURN JOURNEY :   LAST COACH LEAVES **1800** HRS

THIS TICKET MUST BE RETAINED FOR RETURN JOURNEY

550

Another view of the Coronation Review of the Royal Air Force by HM Queen Elizabeth II at RAF Odiham, 15 July 1953. The centre of the static display featured the RAF's training aircraft with numerous Chipmunks, Harvards and Provost aircraft parked in a curve. Also in the photograph are camouflaged Auster and Canberra aircraft, while lines of Vampire and Venom fighters, along with various transport and communications aircraft, extend into the distance. The static display was dominated by the lines of giant Washington bombers, Shackleton patrol aircraft and Hastings transport aircraft. *(Crown Copyright/Air Historical Branch AHB-UNK-Coronation Review-Colour-2)*

The Queen's Colour for the Royal Air Force in the United Kingdom is marched past Her Majesty in slow time to signal the start of the ceremonial parade at the Coronation Review, 15 July 1953. *(Crown Copyright/Air Historical Branch AHB-UNK-Coronation Review-Colour-3)*

▲ HM the Queen, accompanied by the Parade Commander Group Captain R.J.A. Ford CBE, Air Marshal Sir Victor Groom, HRH the Duke of Edinburgh and Air Commodore Sir Edward Fielden, inspecting the parade at the Coronation Review of the Royal Air Force at RAF Odiham on 15 July 1953. *(Crown Copyright/Air Historical Branch AHB-UNK-Coronation Review-Colour-5)*

▼ Hastings and Shackleton crews are seen here lined up with their respective aircraft during the afternoon inspection of the parade by HM the Queen at RAF Odiham on 15 July 1953. *(Crown Copyright/Air Historical Branch AHB-UNK-Coronation Review-Colour-13)*

An aerial view of the Coronation Review of the Royal Air Force. More than 150 aircraft can be seen in this shot of the northern half of the static parade. Included in the lines of aircraft are no fewer than seventy-seven Meteors, twelve Sabres and eight Lincolns, as well as ten Varsities and Valettas. *(Crown Copyright/Air Historical Branch AHB-UNK-Coronation Review-Colour-8)*

◁ Twenty-four Venoms, drawn from squadrons based in Germany with the 2nd Tactical Air Force (2 TAF), complete their flypast over lines of Vampires, Venom FB.1s, Sabres, Washington B.1s, Shackleton MR.1 and MR.2s, Hastings, Ansons and Oxfords at RAF Odiham on 15 July 1953. *(Crown Copyright/ Air Historical Branch X-46600)*

A Another aerial view of the Coronation Review at RAF Odiham on 15 July 1953 as three Washington B.1s from the wing at RAF Marham pass over at precisely 15.49.30 hours, and at 195mph and 1,200ft. They were part of a formation of twelve Washingtons led by Wing Commander H.N.G. Wheeler. *(Crown Copyright/Air Historical Branch AHB-UNK-Coronation Review-Washingtons)*

V The crew of Hastings C.2, WJ327, take the opportunity to view one of five nine-aircraft formations of Avro Lincolns drawn from Bomber Command as they fly over the parade 1,200ft above the airfield. *(Crown Copyright/Air Historical Branch X-46567)*

Russian aggression

On 12 March 1953, seven airmen were killed when the Avro Lincoln B.2 (RF531) they were flying in was shot down by a Soviet fighter in the Berlin air corridor. The airmen, from the RAF Central Gunnery School, were on a training flight. *Flight* magazine reported the incident under the headline 'Russian Aggression' and went on to record:

'what was probably the most serious attack ever made on British life and property in peace-time was the shooting down of a Royal Air Force Lincoln by Russian fighters on Thursday 12 March. The aircraft was one of a number used by Flying Training Command on regular exercises over the Continent, and it had taken off from Leconfield, Yorkshire, earlier in the day.

'At 1:20pm GMT, it was entering the 20-mile-wide international air corridor leading from Hamburg to Berlin at a height given as between 7,000 and 10,000ft. Here, it was attacked, without warning, by two or more fighter aircraft – reported to have been MiG-15s – which opened fire with cannon from close range. The Lincoln went into a steep dive and was followed down by its attacker. At about 3,000ft the bomber's starboard wing caught fire and, shortly afterwards, three of the crew baled out. Finally, the Lincoln broke up at low altitude, the main wreckage landing in a wood on the Russian side of the frontier.

'Of the seven members of the crew, two landed alive, one in the British and one in the Russian Zone, but died shortly afterwards. The bodies of the four, who stayed with the aircraft, were handed over by the Russians last Saturday.'

On 17 March, Winston Churchill made a statement in the House of Commons. After expressing the sympathy of the government and of the House of Commons to the relatives of the seven aircrew who had died, the Prime Minister went on to speak of the 'cruel and wanton attack by Soviet fighter aircraft' on the unarmed Lincoln. He said that:

'on training missions, when not engaged in gunnery practice, our aircraft had hitherto carried no ammunition. The Lincoln's belt-feed mechanism had, in fact, been removed from both Hispano 20mm guns in the upper turret, as was the practice when it was not intended to fire these weapons. The 0.5-inch machine guns in the rear turret were complete, but were not provided with ammunition. The Russians' assertion that the Lincoln opened fire on them is utterly untrue.'

He went on to add:

'A study of the information now available indicated that the aircraft might, through a navigational error, have accidentally crossed into the Eastern Zone of Germany at some point. But the evidence of ground observers, and the spent cannon-shell links from the Russian fighters picked up in our Western Zone, proved that the Russian fighters repeatedly fired on the Lincoln and mercilessly destroyed it when it was actually west of, and within, the Allied zonal frontier. The wreck of the aircraft followed in its descent a track which caused it to fall just within the Russian Zone. Thus, it was actually over our zone when first and mortally fired on, and the lives of seven British airmen were callously taken for a navigational mistake in the process of correction, which could have been dealt with by the usual method of protest and inquiry.'

Shortly afterwards, General Chuikov, head of the Soviet Control Commission in Germany, proposed a conference to discuss the question of air passage through the zones. He rejected as 'incorrect' the British protest about the shooting down of the Lincoln, but it is significant that his statement contained the phrase, 'I regret that the members of the crew of a British bomber lost their lives.'

Overseas operations

During 1953, Britain was still involved with emergencies in Malaya, Korea, Kenya and Oman.

Shortly before the end of 1952, the six-year photographic task performed by 82 Squadron in Africa was completed. It brought to an end one of the largest mapping programmes ever attempted in peacetime. Avro Lancasters had been converted for photography and two Dakotas had been used for passenger- and freight-carrying as well as supply-dropping to parties manning remote radar beacon sites required for accurate navigation. From the photographic survey topographical maps were made for colonial development schemes such as planning a rail link between East and Central

Africa, irrigation projects in Basutoland, hydro-electric schemes in Rhodesia and West Africa, and for plotting international boundaries.

With one constructive task in Africa successfully completed, the RAF was next faced with another more frustrating mission. In November, seven Avro Lincoln B.2 bombers of 49 Squadron were employed in Kenya to strike against the elusive guerrilla groups in the dense jungle. Apart from any psychological value, the bombs did little damage to the Mau Mau. In all, five squadrons were rotated through Eastleigh from 1953 to 1955, with 49 Squadron completing two tours of duty.

Earlier in 1953, Harvard IIB aircraft of 1340 Flight, temporarily detached at Eastleigh from training schools in Rhodesia, operated from an improvised airstrip 8,000ft up in the Kenyan mountains. Each aircraft was fitted with a machine gun and racks for eight 19lb fragmentation bombs, and, helped by reconnaissance reports from Piper Cub aircraft working closely with local security forces, they were able to react to information far more quickly than the bombers.

Perhaps the bombing operations also had a long-term psychological effect of a different kind? For many years after the war ended and after Kenya had gained independence, a young Kenyan boy wrote to the Air Ministry saying he had been much impressed by RAF bombing in the jungle. The operations had succeeded in killing several of his Mau Mau-affiliated relatives, and he had, as a result, developed a burning desire to join the RAF and to learn to fly!

On 27 July 1953, an armistice was signed which became effective at 22.00 hours, which signalled that the Korean War was over. South Korean military casualties were put at 415,000 dead and 249,000 wounded, while the Americans, who bore the brunt of the fighting, lost 33,629 men with 105,785 wounded. The other UN participants lost over 3,000 dead and nearly 12,000 wounded while estimates for the Chinese and North Korean dead range from 1 to 1.5 million. UN Air Forces flew 1,040,708 sorties for the loss of 2,670 aircraft on operations, while North Korea and Chinese losses certainly exceeded 2,200 aircraft. Even to this day North and South Korea technically remain at war, and from time to time there have been a number of border incidents.

▽ On 2 January 1953, the first batch of Canadair-built Sabre F.1 and F.4 aircraft for the RAF were handed over by Mr Norman Robertson, the Canadian High Commissioner, to the Secretary of State for Air, the Lord de l'Isle and Dudley VC, during a ceremony at RAF Abingdon. The Sabre was the RAF's first swept-wing fighter and was acquired as a stop-gap measure until the Hawker Hunter entered service. Many of the 430 Sabres served with Germany-based squadrons. *(Crown Copyright/Air Historical Branch PRB-1-5766)*

⋀ The prototype Handley Page HP.80, WB771 (yet to be named Victor), pictured at Boscombe Down on 6 January 1953, shortly after the aircraft had made its maiden flight. The maximum bomb load of the Victor was 35,000lbs – considerably greater than that of the Vulcan at 21,000lbs. Information at the time suggested that 'production of the Victor had gone ahead despite entrenched opposition by the Treasury which advocated exclusive standardisation on the Vulcan. An early production Victor B.1 cost £820,000, including engines and embodiment loan items, of which some £450,000 covered airframe and flying systems. By comparison a fully-equipped Vulcan B.1 cost £1,002,000.' *(Crown Copyright/Air Historical Branch PRB-1-5773)*

⋁ Three de Havilland Chipmunk T.10s of the Royal Air Force College (WK612/DX, WP838/JA and WP863/JH), are seen here flying past the famous College Hall at RAF Cranwell on 2 February 1953. *(Crown Copyright/Air Historical Branch PRB-1-5828)*

△ A servicing party swarm around the prototype Canberra PR.3, VX181, after its arrival at Changi, Singapore, during a record-breaking 22-hour flight from London–Darwin on 28 January 1953. Having landed at Changi with only 150 gallons of fuel on board, the aircraft was refuelled and started the final leg of the flight just 53 minutes later. The aircraft, piloted by Flight Lieutenant L.M. 'Dick' Whittington with Flight Lieutenant J.M. Brown, also set a record time for London–Karachi of 8 hours 52 minutes. *(Crown Copyright/Air Historical Branch CFP-688)*

➤ Two versions of the Shackleton maritime patrol aircraft flying with 42 Squadron at RAF St Eval, photographed on 25 June 1953. Nearest the camera is WG527/A-D, a MR.1A, while an unidentified MR.2 (coded 'B') flies in loose formation. *(Crown Copyright/Air Historical Branch PRB-1-5876)*

Three Canadair Sabre F.4s of the Ferry Training Unit at RAF Abingdon, photographed in formation on 10 March 1953. The aircraft – XB537/E, XB543/G and XB545/J – were among the first delivered to the UK in December 1952 and were being used to train pilots for the forthcoming Operation Becher's Brook, in which 430 Sabre F.1 and F.4s were ferried to the UK via Labrador, Greenland and Iceland (see also pages 107 and 123). *(Crown Copyright/Air Historical Branch PRB-1-6017)*

Three de Havilland Vampire T.11 two-seat training aircraft – WZ456/29, WZ457/21 and WZ453/20 – photographed in formation on 20 April 1953, shortly after being delivered to 208 Advanced Flying School at RAF Merryfield. *(Crown Copyright/Air Historical Branch PRB-1-6155)*

⋏ Avro Shackleton MR.2s of 42 Squadron photographed flying over Durban on 22 April 1953 during a visit to South Africa. The squadron was undertaking a tour to the Far East which covered 17,740 miles in April and May of 1953. *(Crown Copyright/Air Historical Branch CFP-744)*

⋎ In May 1953, Handley Page Hastings C.2, WD499, of the Royal Air Force Flying College at RAF Manby, was used for an arctic training flight over the North Pole. The aircraft is pictured here on the arctic ice cap before setting out for the top of the world. *(Crown Copyright/Air Historical Branch PRB-1-6251)*

▲ Four of the first Sabre F.4s to serve with the 2nd Tactical Air Force being refuelled at Wildenrath, Germany, after a sortie in May 1953. All four aircraft (XB542, XB592, XB603 plus one unidentified example) had been delivered to the Sabre Conversion Flight in March and April 1953 to train pilots on the new swept-wing fighter. XB603 was written off on 15 June when the pilot misjudged his landing at Wildenrath and stalled. *(Crown Copyright/Air Historical Branch PRB-1-6313)*

◄ Four de Havilland Venom FB.1s of 11 Squadron loop in formation during a sortie from Wunstorf, Germany, in May 1953. The squadron was the first to receive the Venom – an improved version of the Vampire – in mid-1952. *(Crown Copyright/Air Historical Branch PRB-1-6343)*

▲ Twenty-four Meteors of the Biggin Hill Wing gathered on the runway at their home station on 12 May 1953 while rehearsing for the RAF Coronation flypast due to be held on 2 June 1953. A total of 168 fighters (144 Meteors accompanied by 24 Sabres of the Royal Canadian Air Force) were scheduled to fly over Pall Mall following the Queen's Coronation but sadly this had to be cancelled due to the poor weather on the day. *(Crown Copyright/Air Historical Branch PRB-1-6361)*

▼ A week later than the photograph above, on 19 May, twenty Meteors of Fighter Command formed up over the Kent countryside during rehearsals for the Coronation flypast on 2 June. Sadly, their efforts were in vain too, owing to the unpredictable British weather. *(Crown Copyright/Air Historical Branch PRB-1-6410)*

A flight of four Meteor NF.11s of 256 Squadron based at Ahlhorn, Germany, May 1953. Two of the aircraft, WD631 and WD698, were sold to France in 1954. *(Crown Copyright/Air Historical Branch PRB-1-6397)*

➤ Lockheed Neptune MR.1, WX505/A-J, of 217 Squadron peels away from the camera aircraft during a training flight from RAF Kinloss on 28 May 1953. *(Crown Copyright/Air Historical Branch PRB-1-6502)*

▲ Armourers at Tengah, Singapore, prepare 1,000lb bombs before they are loaded into a waiting Lincoln B.2 of 57 Squadron (RF386/DX-N) for an anti-communist strike in the Malayan jungle during Operation Firedog, 2 May 1953. *(Crown Copyright/Air Historical Branch CFP-721)*

▼ The prototype Handley Page Victor, WB771, pictured in mid-1953. The aircraft is still in its original natural metal finish, but for its debut at the 1953 SBAC Farnborough Air Show, a striking black and red scheme was applied (see page 114). *(Crown Copyright/Air Historical Branch PRB-1-6824)*

Ⲁ An unusual mixed formation of aircraft used by the Central Flying School Examining Wing based at RAF Little Rissington in July 1953. None of the aircraft were on the permanent strength of the wing, each being loaned by their parent unit as required. From right to left, are: Avro Shackleton MR.1A, WB831/L-D (220 Squadron, RAF Kinloss); Gloster Meteor T.7, WA630/W (205 Advanced Flying School, RAF Middleton St George); de Havilland Vampire T.11, WZ576/35 (208 Advanced Flying School, RAF Merryfield); Vickers Varsity T.1, WJ892/Q (1 Air Navigation School, RAF Hullavington); Canadair Sabre F.4, XB547 (Ferry Training Unit, RAF Abingdon); plus an unidentified Boulton Paul Balliol T.2 coded Q-X (from 7 Flying Training School at RAF Cottesmore). *(Crown Copyright/Air Historical Branch PRB-1-6724)*

Ⲩ To aid the development of the Vulcan, Avro built five half-scale aerodynamic test aircraft known as the Avro 707. Three versions were built, the Type 707A, B and C, each with differing aerodynamic characteristics and wing shapes. The sole Type 707C, WZ744, seen here at around the time of the 1953 SBAC Show at Farnborough, had a two-seat cockpit with side-by-side seating and dual controls. WZ744 is now preserved at the RAF Museum, Cosford. *(Crown Copyright/Air Historical Branch PRB-1-6805)*

➤ Percival Provost T.1s of the Central Flying School, based at RAF South Cerney, break from echelon starboard formation during a sortie over southern England on 6 August 1953. The aircraft are (from front to back): WV423, WV431, WV432, WV438 and WV430. *(Crown Copyright/Air Historical Branch PRB-1-6761)*

Pioneer STOL aircraft enters RAF service

Powered by an Alvis Leonides radial engine developing 520hp, the prototype Scottish Aviation Pioneer made its first flight in June 1950. Under the designation Pioneer CC.1, it was adopted by the RAF for operations in rough and restricted territories such as the Malayan jungle, the Aden Protectorate and in Cyprus. It entered service in August 1953 with 267 Squadron at Kuala Lumpur – part of the Far East Air Force (FEAF) – where they played an important role in the Firedog operations against terrorists, flying on internal security work and keeping the far-flung jungle forts supplied. Forty were supplied to the RAF before production ceased in February 1957.

SBAC Show Highlights

The highlight of the SBAC Show at Farnborough held from 5–11 September was undoubtedly the formation of two Avro Vulcan aircraft along with four of the Avro 707 research aircraft used so successfully in the Vulcan's development programme. The strikingly painted prototype Handley Page Victor B.1 (WB771) made its first appearance at the event, marking the first occasion that all three V-bombers were present at Farnborough.

Having displayed the prototype 'Universal Transport' at the previous year's SBAC Air Show, Blackburn displayed the second prototype, now known as the Beverley C.1, at the 1953 event. The aircraft, WZ889, waits at the end of Farnborough's runway to commence its flying display. *(Crown Copyright/Air Historical Branch PRB-1-6848a)*

A striking head-on image of the prototype Avro Vulcan taken en route to the SBAC Show at Farnborough in September 1953. Having originally been fitted with four Rolls-Royce Avon engines, the aircraft was now powered by four Armstrong Siddeley Sapphires, which increased the total available thrust from the original 26,000lb up to 32,000lb. *(Crown Copyright/Air Historical Branch PRB-1-6851)*

Two views of the strikingly painted prototype Handley Page Victor, WB771, now painted with a black fuselage and red cheat line. These shots were taken during the SBAC Show at Farnborough in September 1953. *(Above: Crown Copyright/Air Historical Branch PRB-1-6850; below: Crown Copyright/Air Historical Branch PRB-1-6850b)*

The Boulton Paul P.111 experimental delta-wing aircraft is pictured here after having received a redesigned wing and tail along with other modifications to the airframe, all incorporated while the aircraft was being rebuilt following an earlier accident at Boscombe Down in August 1952. Now redesignated as the P.111A, this aircraft, VT935, was photographed en route to its appearance at the 1953 SBAC Show at Farnborough. *(Above: Crown Copyright/Air Historical Branch PRB-1-6853; below: Crown Copyright/Air Historical Branch PRB-1-6857)*

▲ The sole Avro 707C dual-control delta-winged research aircraft, WZ744, extends its air brakes for the photographer while en route to appear at the SBAC Show at Farnborough in September 1953. Originally built as part of the Vulcan development programme, WZ744 was used to train pilots in the properties of delta-wing aircraft. It was later used by the Royal Aircraft Establishment in the development of fly-by-wire control systems before reaching the end of its useful life in 1966. The aircraft is now part of the RAF Museum Collection and is exhibited at Cosford. *(Crown Copyright/Air Historical Branch PRB-1-6854)*

▼ The pilot of the second prototype Blackburn B.101 Universal Freighter 2 (later named the Beverley), WZ889, nudges the huge transport closer to the camera-ship for this head-on photograph. The aircraft also carried the civilian registration G-AMVW. A total of forty-seven Beverley C.1s served with transport squadrons across the RAF between 1956 and 1968. At the time of the photograph it was the largest aircraft operated by the RAF and was the first capable of air-dropping outsize loads by parachute through the rear doors, which were usually removed for the purpose. *(Crown Copyright/Air Historical Branch PRB-1-6855)*

One of several experimental aircraft on show at the SBAC Air Show at Farnborough in September 1953 was the unique Short SB.5, WG768. It was produced to meet a specification to research the handling characteristics of aircraft with sharply swept wings at low speeds. Its wings could be adjusted to allow three different sweep angles – 50°, 60° (as pictured) or 69° – while on the ground and it also had an adjustable tailplane. It was later rebuilt to reflect the wing layout of the Lightning supersonic fighter then under development. The aircraft was allocated the maintenance serial 8002M and is now exhibited with the Royal Air Force Museum at Cosford. *(Crown Copyright/Air Historical Branch PRB-1-6856)*

During the 1953 SBAC Air Show at Farnborough, Avro took the opportunity to highlight its delta-wing aircraft programme by flying the first two Vulcan prototypes. VX777 is seen here leading, with VX770 behind, in formation with four of the half-scale Avro 707 aerodynamic research aircraft – two Type 707As (WD280 and WZ736) along with one each of the 707B (VX790) and 707C (WZ744). *(Crown Copyright/Air Historical Branch PRB-1-6865)*

⋀ Handley Page Marathon T.11, XA274, based at the RAF Flying College, Manby (with the Handling Squadron), photographed in flight on 24 September 1953. In 1951 the Air Ministry decided to adopt the Marathon as a navigation trainer for the RAF. After trials with the prototype T.11 (VX229) the first of twenty-eight Marathons for the RAF (XA249-XA276) made its maiden flight on 29 August 1952. After a relatively short career, all Marathons were finally withdrawn from RAF service in June 1958. *(Crown Copyright/ Air Historical Branch PRB-1-6922)*

⋁ Many of the newer aircraft entering service with the RAF and Royal Navy were delivered to the Handling Squadron at the Flying College, RAF Manby, for final pre-service checks before being issued to front-line squadrons or for trials for those already in service. The mixed formation shown here consists of some of the aircraft flying with the unit in September 1953. The lead section, from right to left, consists of the Avro Athena, Percival Pembroke and Handley Page Marathon. The second section comprises three naval aircraft: the Westland Wyvern, Supermarine Attacker and Hawker Sea Hawk, while the rear formation has a de Havilland Vampire T.11, Gloster Meteor NF.11 and an English Electric Canberra. *(Crown Copyright/Air Historical Branch PRB-1-6938)*

London–New Zealand Air Race

After Christchurch took the decision to declare their airport as 'International' in 1953, a London to Christchurch air race was declared to promote the event. Billed as 'The Last Great Air Race', the course from London International Airport at Heathrow to Christchurch International Airport was 12,270 miles in length and the race took place from the 8–10 October.

The race, supervised by the Royal Aero Club, was divided into two sections: an outright speed section and another for commercial aircraft. Five military Canberra aircraft entered; three from the RAF's 540 Squadron at RAF Wyton (two PR.3s – WE142 and WE139; and a single PR.7 – WH773), along with a pair of B.20s from the Royal Australian Air Force's (RAAF) No 1 Long Range Flight – A84-201 and 202. There were only three entrants in the commercial aircraft section – a KLM (Royal Dutch Airlines) DC-6A (PH-TGA), a British European Airways (BEA) Vickers Viscount (G-AMAV) and a Royal New Zealand Air Force (RNZAF) Hastings (NZ5804).

The speed section was won by a Canberra PR.3, WE139, flown by Flight Lieutenant R.L.E. Burton, with Flight Lieutenant D.H. Gannon as navigator. They covered the 12,270 miles in 23 hours, 50 minutes and 42 seconds in the air, including 83 minutes on the ground; a record that still stands. It also established a London–Shaibah record of 5 hours, 11 minutes and 5.6 seconds at 544.3mph (876km/h). RAF Canberra aircraft also set two other point-to-point records for London–Basra (Iraq) and London–Colombo (Ceylon). Second in this section was the RAAF Canberra B.20 A84-201, flown by Squadron Leader Peter Raw, with Canberra PR.3 WE142 in third. WE139 is currently preserved in the RAF Museum at Hendon.

The commercial aircraft section was won by the Vickers Viscount, securing the first prize of £10,000 with a handicap time of 44 hours, 29 minutes and 31 seconds. The KLM DC-6A was second, while the RNZAF Hastings was forced to withdraw after suffering engine problems in Ceylon.

Entrants for the 1953 London–Christchurch Air Race – billed as the 'Last Great Air Race' – lined up at London Airport in October 1953. A mixed entry of six military aircraft (two RAAF Canberra B.20s, one RNZAF Hastings, two RAF Canberra PR.3s and a single Canberra PR.7) competed against a Douglas DC-6 of KLM and a BEA Viscount on a handicap basis. The winner was declared as Flight Lieutenant Roland Burton flying the second of the 540 Squadron Canberra PR.3s (WE139), who reached Christchurch in a record time of 23 hours, 50 minutes and 42 seconds. *(Crown Copyright/Air Historical Branch PRB-1-6988)*

The RAF's last Wellington

The RAF's last Wellington made its farewell service flight in October 1953. The aircraft, a T.10, MF628, was one of 270 Mark X bombers refurbished by Boulton Paul as aircrew trainers, and delivered to 1 Air Navigation School at Hullavington in April 1949. MF628 remained with the unit until 28 October 1952 when it was flown to St Athan and placed in store. Having been kept in airworthy condition, MF628 took part in several flypasts during 1953 and was used as a camera-ship during the making of the *The Dam Busters* film at Hemswell in 1954. The aircraft is now preserved at the RAF Museum, Hendon.

V The RAF's last Wellington, pictured just before its farewell flight in October 1953. The aircraft, a T.10, MF628, was one of 270 Mark X bombers refurbished by Boulton Paul as aircrew trainers and delivered to 1 Air Navigation School at RAF Hullavington in April 1949. MF628 remained with the unit until 28 October 1952 when it was flown to St Athan and placed in store. MF628 took part in several flypasts in 1953 and was used as a camera-ship for the film *The Dam Busters* during 1954. The aircraft is now preserved at the RAF Museum, Hendon. *(Crown Copyright/Air Historical Branch PRB-1-7026)*

Four de Havilland Vampire FB.5s – VV555/70, VV556/72, VV688/58 and VZ224/42 – of the 208 Advanced Flying School aerobatic team. Based at RAF Merryfield, they performed over their Somerset home during Battle of Britain Week, September 1953. The team comprised Flight Lieutenants Tim Greenfield and Rob Batten, along with Pilot Officers Alec Cornish and S. Edwards. *(Left: Crown Copyright/Air Historical Branch PRB-1-6996; below: Crown Copyright/Air Historical Branch PRB-1-6997)*

The Meteor T.7 Aerobatic Team of 203 Advanced Flying School, RAF Driffield, which performed before HRH the Duke of Edinburgh at a graduation parade at the RAF College Cranwell, 28 July 1953. The team, consisting of Meteor T.7s WL413/X-68, WF881/X-55, WF776/X-54 and WL361/X-71, were photographed in flight shortly before being disbanded in October of that year. *(Right: Crown Copyright/Air Historical Branch PRB-1-7011; below: Crown Copyright/Air Historical Branch PRB-1-7013)*

A A line of twenty-eight Canadair Sabre F.4s sitting at Goose Bay, Labrador, during one of the numerous ferry flights undertaken between Canada and the UK as part of Operation Becher's Brook. The 3,100-mile flights via Goose Bay, Greenland, Iceland and Prestwick, could take anything from two days to three weeks depending on the weather. All were flown by specially trained crews from 147 Squadron. *(Crown Copyright/Air Historical Branch PRB-1-7033)*

V A group of Canadair Sabre F.4s, having recently been ferried across the North Atlantic, are seen here at 5 Maintenance Unit at RAF Kemble in October 1953. Here the aircraft were camouflaged and readied for squadron service. The two aircraft nearest the camera, XB669 and XB733, were issued to Nos 71 and 4 Squadrons in October 1953 and March 1954 respectively. Interestingly, both were to have flying accidents in mid-1954 and both were placed in store in 1955; XB669 returned to the US Air Force in June 1956 and XB733 followed in May 1957. *(Crown Copyright/Air Historical Branch PRB-1-7063)*

▲ An interesting formation of aircraft belonging to the Central Fighter Establishment at RAF West Raynham, photographed on 12 November 1953. From left to right are a Meteor NF.11 (WD798), Venom NF.2 (WL818), Sabre F.4 (XB666), Meteor T.7 (unidentified), Vampire FB.1 (WE313) and Meteor F.8 (WK943). Two Royal Navy fighters completed the formation and are positioned furthest from the camera – a Supermarine Attacker and Hawker Sea Hawk. *(Crown Copyright/Air Historical Branch PRB-1-7163)*

▼ Three RAF officers who flew an English Electric Canberra of Bomber Command through the 'atomic cloud' just six-and-a-half minutes after the explosion of an atomic weapon at the Woomera Range, Australia. It was the first time such a flight had been made so soon after an atomic explosion. The crew are (left to right): Wing Commander E.W. Anderson (Navigator), Wing Commander G. Dhenin (Pilot, Medical Officer) and Group Captain D.A. Wilson (Observer, Medical Officer). The nose art on the aircraft shows the white swan of England and green fields facing across the sea with the black swan of Australia on desert sand, centred by the badge of the Medical Branch of the RAF. *(Crown Copyright/Air Historical Branch PRB-1-7187)*

Farewell to the Lancaster bomber

The last Avro Lancaster flying with Bomber Command, PA427/M, was retired from service in December 1953. Manufactured to Far East Air Force standards, PA427 was delivered straight into storage at 38 Maintenance Unit at Llandow, Glamorgan, in July 1945. It was eventually issued to 230 OCU at Lindholme in August 1948 before joining 49 Squadron at Waddington a year later. At the end of 1950, PA427 was converted for the photo-reconnaissance role before spending a further year in storage at Wroughton. In May 1952 the aircraft joined 82 Squadron at Benson, which was undertaking a photographic survey of East Africa. In December 1953 the aircraft was returned to Llandow for a further period in store and was eventually sold for scrap in February 1955.

The last Avro Lancaster flying with Bomber Command, PA427/M, was retired from service in December 1953. Delivered straight into storage at 38 Maintenance Unit at Llandow, Glamorgan, in July 1945, the aircraft was eventually issued to 230 OCU at Lindholme in August 1948 before joining 49 Squadron at Waddington a year later. When this photograph was taken on 2 December 1953, the aircraft was days away from its final flight back to Llandow for a further period in store. It was eventually sold as scrap in February 1955. *(Above: Crown Copyright/Air Historical Branch PRB-1-7277; below: Crown Copyright/Air Historical Branch PRB-1-7278)*

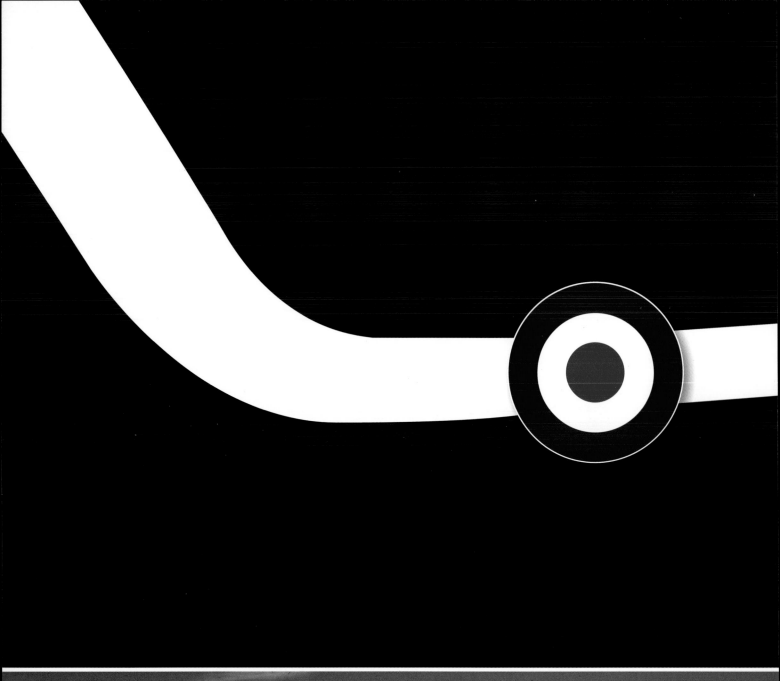

1954

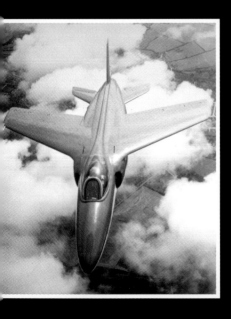

Overshadowing all else in 1954 was the emergence of the thermonuclear bomb. It was in 1954 that official information was first released by the US Government on the experimental explosion of a weapon at Eniwetok (which had taken place in November 1952) that was several hundred times more powerful than the atomic bombs dropped on Hiroshima and Nagasaki in 1945. On 1 March, an even more powerful thermonuclear weapon was tested in the Marshall Islands. At the time, it was stated that there were no technical or scientific limitations on the production of nuclear weapons of even greater size and devastation.

The Government of the United States announced they were proceeding with full-scale production of thermonuclear weapons. The Soviet Union was clearly following the same policy, although it was not known at the time just how soon they might have such weapons ready for operational use. The UK also had the ability to produce them and after considering all of the implications, and despite the difficult financial conditions, the government decided to proceed with their development and production. 'To fail to maintain our defence effort up to the limit of our strength,' Sir Winston Churchill said, 'would be to paralyse every beneficial tendency towards peace, both in Europe and Asia.'

➤ **Having had a long-term interest in the security of Egypt, and in particular of the Suez Canal, Britain still had assets based in that country in 1954. A flight of four de Havilland Vampire FB.9s of 213 Squadron were photographed in flight from their base at Deversoir, Egypt, in that year. The FB.9 was the tropicalised version of the Vampire for use in 'hot and high' climates such as the Middle East and North Africa.** *(Crown Copyright/Air Historical Branch image T-6)*

At the time, Britain was also in the process of providing a modernised defence system including an improved control and reporting capability, all-weather radar-equipped fighters, as well as air-to-air and ground-to-air guided weapons. As part of this programme, the first British swept-wing fighter, the Supermarine Swift, entered service in February, with the Hawker Hunter entering service in July. By the end of 1954, delivery of North American Sabre F.1 and F.4s was almost complete and the air-to-air guided weapon which was expected to increase their effectiveness by a factor of four was just around the corner.

In July 1954, with the RAF overseas forces engaged in a wide variety of operations, RAF Fighter Command in the UK was carrying out the biggest air defence exercise since the war. Code-named Dividend, its object was to practice defence against nuclear attack. Around 6,000 bomber sorties were flown against targets in the UK by aircraft from Bomber Command, USAF bombers from Europe and the Fleet Air Arm, as well as Flying Training Command. The NATO control and reporting systems were closely coordinated with the UK system throughout the exercise, as it would be in times of war. On the defence side, some 80,000 men and women were engaged, including Regular and Auxiliary fighter squadrons, control and reporting units, Royal Observer Corps and anti-aircraft units.

Exercise Dividend clearly confirmed that the UK air defence and NATO air defence were intrinsically linked. The NATO early warning system in Europe had made it possible to scramble UK fighters in time to intercept 'enemy' bombers up to 100 miles from the English coast. In the following year, the air defence of the NATO area was closely coordinated between the Southern Region (which included Turkey, Greece and Italy), the Central Region (which included Germany, Holland, Belgium, Luxembourg and France) and the Northern Region (Norway, Denmark and the UK).

During exercise Battle Royal, held in the autumn of 1954, 2nd TAF in Germany was given the opportunity of testing its operational efficiency in realistic conditions and its reconnaissance capability in particular. RAF Meteor FR.9 (fighter reconnaissance) and PR.10 (photo-reconnaissance) aircraft, along with Canberra PR.9 aircraft utilised for high-altitude photography over longer ranges, operated at full stretch alongside F-84 Thunderjets of the Dutch and Belgian air forces. Exercise Dividend clearly demonstrated that although the 2nd TAF had been reasonably successful in finding and reporting targets, its reconnaissance capability was still severely limited in bad weather. It was evident from the exercise that more and better radar would be required to overcome this dangerous shortcoming.

Although the jet aircraft had certainly arrived by 1954, some of the older piston-engined warhorses were still performing a valuable service in the RAF. Four maritime reconnaissance Shackleton aircraft from Coastal Command's No 206 Squadron carried out a 40,000-mile flight to the Far East in the latter part of 1954. Here, they participated in maritime exercises in the Indian Ocean off Ceylon. While in the area, they made goodwill and training visits to Australia, New Zealand and Fiji. The visit of these aircraft to the Far East coincided with the signing, in September 1954, of a collective defence treaty for the South-East Asia area. With their signatures, the governments of France, New Zealand, Pakistan, the Philippines, Siam, the UK and the US, gave further evidence of the desire among many of the need for goodwill to unite for mutual protection.

One event that occurred in 1954 is worthy of special mention as, at the time, the significance for the future could not have been fully appreciated. In the autumn of 1954 six Canberra B.2 aircraft from 57 Squadron at Cottesmore had visited Iraq, Jordan and Tripolitania in the course of a training and goodwill flight. This was to be the last occasion on which so complete a tour of Arab States would be politically feasible.

Reorganising the reserves

Following Dividend, it was recognised that the threat of nuclear attack would continue to present problems to the UK air defence forces, although the expansion of Fighter Command was almost complete. Later in the year, the Minster of Defence, Harold Macmillan, referred in parliament to the anti-aircraft gun defences of the UK. The development of nuclear weapons and long-range aircraft operating at high speed and high altitude had significantly reduced the effectiveness of anti-aircraft defences. Some heavy and light anti-aircraft regiments were retained to defend field forces and certain vital targets, but did not justify the retention of Anti-Aircraft Command.

At the time, the government also took the opportunity to alter the organisation of the Royal Auxiliary Air Force (RAuxAF). After paying tribute to 'the high tradition and glorious record' of the RAuxAF, Harold Macmillan went on to describe why it would 'not be possible for the

Auxiliary squadrons, if they are re-equipped with the swept-wing aircraft, [Sabre, Swift and Hunter] to train to a standard high enough to enable them to take their place in the frontline, as squadrons, immediately on the outbreak of war, and that is what all fighter squadrons must be required to do in present conditions, because they are needed at the very first moment. So an effective fighter squadron of modern aircraft must really be a whole-time duty'.

The government decided not to re-equip the RAuxAF with modern swept-wing fighters; instead it chose to reorganise the force so that those pilots who could give the time could be trained on the new fighters at other facilities. By organising the Auxiliary squadrons in this way, they would provide reserves behind a Regular squadron in war. Each squadron was linked with a Regular squadron and Auxiliary pilots flew the aircraft of the Regular squadrons. The Auxiliary squadrons retained their town headquarters as well as their resident airfield; each squadron also retained a training flight composed of Meteor or Vampire aircraft. They could then fly those aircraft to the Regular airfields for training on swept-wing jets, as required.

Overseas operations

In 1954, Britain was still involved in emergencies in Malaya, Kenya and Oman, while still maintaining an internal security force in the Suez Canal Zone of Egypt.

In the Kenya Emergency, some 20,000 Mau Mau had been killed or captured by the end of 1954, but it was thought that at least a further 7,000 of the tenacious hardcore terrorists were still at liberty.

A number of RAF aircraft were operating from Nairobi. Six Avro Lincoln B.2s were placed on detachment from their home bases in the UK, the task in 1954 being shared between Nos 100 and 61 Squadrons. Four Vampire FB.9s from 8 Squadron and two Meteor PR.10s from 13 Squadron were also detached to Eastleigh from their bases in Aden. These supported the 1340 Flight Harvard IIBs operating in the ground-attack role. An Auster AOP.6, and later a Pembroke C.1 from the Communications Flight, operated from Nairobi with sky-shouting equipment for propaganda in the Kikuyu language.

Meanwhile, in Malaya, an aircraft new to the RAF – the Scottish Aviation Pioneer CC.1 – was making a name for itself. Perhaps somewhat surprisingly, the Pioneer CC.1 had not carried out any service trials before entering service with the RAF in the Far East. Its great virtue was

its spectacular short take-off and landing capability. The 520hp Alvis Leonides radial engine, working in conjunction with the high-lift wing design, allowed it to clear a 50ft obstacle in only 180 yards under temperate conditions. Operating from Kuala Lumpur, the Pioneers were successfully employed in flying relief garrisons to remote Malayan jungle forts.

During the summer of 1954 and within the same theatre of operations, Valetta C.1 aircraft of 52 Squadron of the Far East Transport Wing, supported by a Transport Command Hastings, established a record for the amount of supplies dropped by parachute in twenty-four hours to security ground forces operating in many parts of the Federation. The twenty-one dropping zones included jungle forts and Special Air Service unit camps, and the 200 'parapacks' dropped included fresh food supplies, fuel and ammunition for police posts, Gurkha, Malay and British units as well as the King's African Rifles. Equipment for constructing airstrips was also delivered.

Operations against EOKA terrorists

Subject to Turkish sovereignty until the First World War, Cyprus was annexed by Britain in 1914 and became a colony in 1925. With 80 per cent of the population being of Greek origin, pressure grew for Enosis, or amalgamation with Greece. Having recognised the difficulty in getting Britain to concede such an important base, the National Organisation of Cypriot Fighters (EOKA), under the leadership of the ex-Greek colonel George Grivas, resorted to arms. On 1 April 1955, a bombing campaign commenced with attacks on government buildings at Larnaca, Limassol and Nicosia. There was already a large British Army presence on the island following the withdrawal from Egypt in 1954 and, in May 1955, a Sycamore helicopter flight was formed. Its initial role was that of search and rescue while based at Nicosia. After further attacks in the autumn, in which policemen and servicemen were killed, Field Marshal Sir John Harding arrived on the island as governor. Shortly afterwards, a state of emergency was declared on 27 November 1955.

Immediately, the number of troops was increased and the Sycamore flight split to provide an internal security unit. From late 1955, operations Foxhunter, Pepperpot and Lucky Alphonse were mounted in a vain attempt to locate and arrest Grivas and his supporters. The emergency was to continue right up to 1959.

⋀ A flight of three de Havilland Hornet F.3 fighters (WB876/OB-O, WB908/OB-L and WF959/OB-K) of 45 Squadron in flight over the Malayan jungle in February 1954. *(Crown Copyright/Air Historical Branch image CFP-799)*

Farewell to the MR Lancaster

The very last operational maritime reconnaissance Avro Lancaster GR.3 – RF273/T of 38 Squadron based at RAF Luqa, Malta – made its final flight when it took off from the island on 3 February 1954 on its flight back to the UK. 38 Squadron had taken delivery of its first Shackleton MR.2 aircraft in September 1953 and initially operated the two types of aircraft side-by-side. After the retirement of the Lancaster, 38 Squadron continued to operate the Shackleton MR.2 until the squadron was finally disbanded in March 1967.

⋁ A rather grainy but historically significant image of the last operational maritime reconnaissance Lancaster serving with the RAF – RF273/T, a GR.3 of 38 Squadron – taking off from Luqa, Malta, at the start of its final flight back to the UK on 3 February 1954. *(Crown Copyright/Air Historical Branch image CMP-632)*

Farewell to the Spitfire

In early 1954, 81 Squadron was the last operational Spitfire squadron in the RAF – a photographic reconnaissance squadron of the Far East Air Force based in Malaya with a detachment in Hong Kong – when they re-equipped with the Gloster Meteor PR.10. The very last operational Spitfire PR.19 flight was made by an 81 Squadron aircraft on 1 April 1954. The last few months' work of Far East Spitfires constituted a worthy record, for between them they flew 800 photographic reconnaissance sorties in the Malayan anti-bandit campaign. The only remaining Spitfires, fewer than fifty of them, were those used by the then Civil Anti-Aircraft Co-operation Units, which also made the daily meteorological climb from RAF Woodvale.

Supermarine Spitfire PR.19, PS836, of 81 Squadron, seen over a coastal region of Malaya in March 1954, during one of the final operational flights by the type. At this time, 81 Squadron was converting to the Gloster Meteor PR.10 and retired its Spitfires in April 1954. *(Crown Copyright/Air Historical Branch image CFP-845)*

The third prototype Gloster Javelin FAW.1, WT827, photographed during a test flight in early 1954. The aircraft had made its first flight on 7 March 1953 and was the first Javelin to carry the armament of four 30mm Aden guns. A series of accidents with the prototypes delayed the introduction of the type into service, but the first were issued to No 46 Squadron at RAF Odiham in February 1956. *(Crown Copyright/Air Historical Branch image PRB-1-7413)*

➤ The prototype of the English Electric Canberra PR.3 photo-reconnaissance aircraft, VX181. The design was very similar to the B.2 version, but had special cameras installed and its fuselage had been lengthened from 65ft 6in to 66ft 8in to accommodate additional internal fuel tanks. It was due to replace Mosquito PR.34 and PR.35 aircraft which had remained in squadron service after the war. *(Crown Copyright/Air Historical Branch image PRB-1-7424)*

Bristol Brigand B.1, RH798, served at Boscombe Down from new in 1948 until it was transferred to the Ministry of Supply in 1949 for return to the manufacturer and conversion into the prototype Brigand T.4. After conversion, it was then delivered to the Telecommunications Research Establishment (TRE) at Defford in August 1950. In June 1952, RH798 was transferred to 238 OCU at RAF Colerne. By late 1956 all T.4s still in service were flown to Cambridge for conversion by Marshalls to T.5 standard. In June 1957, 238 OCU moved to RAF North Luffenham, where it was finally disbanded in March 1958, after having trained some 600 radar navigators on Brigands. *(Crown Copyright/Air Historical Branch image PRB-1-7434)*

WG259, a Vickers Valetta T.3 navigational training aircraft, photographed in flight on 22 March 1954. The Valetta T.3 was a 'flying classroom' version of the Valetta transport design. It was used to train navigators, hence the line of six astrodomes fitted to the upper fuselage. As such, the T.3 served with five Air Navigation Schools as well as the RAF College at Cranwell. WG259 made its first flight on 27 August 1951 and was delivered to 2 Air Navigation School at RAF Thorney Island on 3 October 1951 where it operated as 'A'. The aircraft was eventually struck off charge in June 1968 and sent to RAF Tangmere for firefighting practice. *(Crown Copyright/Air Historical Branch image PRB-1-7578)*

Transport handling activities at RAF Lyneham in 1954 with a Hastings C.2 (WJ338/GAC) and Valetta C.1 (VL280) photographed in formation on 8 April 1954. The letters 'GAC' worn by the Hastings refer to the aircraft's radio call sign. Valetta C.1 VL280 had made its first flight in September 1948 and operated with a variety of units including the Ferry Training Unit and No 167 Squadron at RAF Benson. VL280 was scrapped in April 1959. *(Crown Copyright/Air Historical Branch image PRB-1-7808)*

A two-seat Vampire T.11 trainer leads out a flight of 6 Squadron Vampire FB.9s (WG889/T, nearest) for a training sortie from Amman, Jordan, in early April 1954. *(Crown Copyright/Air Historical Branch image PRB-1-7873)*

With the end of the Spitfire's operational service drawing ever closer, increasing numbers were being flown to maintenance units to await their final fate. Twenty-four Spitfires can be seen parked outside the hangars of 33 Maintenance Unit at RAF Lyneham in this picture taken during April 1954. *(Crown Copyright/Air Historical Branch image PRB-1-7909a)*

Four de Havilland Vampire FB.9s – WL608/U, WR251, WL586 and WL610 – all of 8 Squadron, return from an anti-bandit strike using rocket projectiles in April 1954. The aircraft are seen at an altitude of 16,000ft over Mau Mau country, with Mount Kenya in the background. *(Crown Copyright/Air Historical Branch image PRB-1-8148)*

Avro Anson C.19 communications aircraft, VM331, of the Aden Protectorate Support Flight at Khormaksar, pictured on a rough landing strip approximately 3 miles from the Aden Protectorate encampment at Dhala, April 1954. *(Crown Copyright/Air Historical Branch image PRB-1-8166)*

Λ Canberra B.2 jet bombers of 27 Squadron (including WH732) which toured Europe and the Mediterranean under the command of Squadron Leader D.H. Chopping DFC, photographed at RAF Scampton on 25 April 1954. 27 Squadron equipped with the Canberra B.2 in June 1953 and retained the type until the squadron was disbanded in December 1957. *(Crown Copyright/ Air Historical Branch image PRB-1-8190)*

➤ Two of the five RAF Sunderland flying boats of the Far East Air Force fly past the SS *Gothic* in salute to HM the Queen in the Indian Ocean as the vessel approached Ceylon for a Commonwealth visit from 10–21 April 1954. In the background is HMS *Ceylon*. *(Crown Copyright/Air Historical Branch image PRB-1-8209)*

A Hunting Percival Provost T.1, WV429/ZN, flies alongside a de Havilland Vampire T.11 trainer, XD520, on 9 June 1954. The Provost was from 6 Flying Training School at RAF Ternhill while the Vampire came from 206 Advanced Flying School based at RAF Oakington. *(Crown Copyright/Air Historical Branch image T-10)*

Gloster Meteor NF.14, WS744, of 85 Squadron, based at RAF West Malling. The NF.14 was one of the night fighter versions of the Meteor, distinguishable by their elongated noses to house the air radar equipment. 85 Squadron operated the NF.14 alongside the NF.12 version from April 1954 to November 1958. *(Crown Copyright/Air Historical Branch image T-27)*

⋀ Another image of an NF.14, probably taken during the same sortie. This time Gloster Meteor NF.14, WS723, of 85 Squadron, is the subject of the photograph. The RAF ordered 100 of each of the NF.12 and NF.14 versions of the Meteor. *(Crown Copyright/ Air Historical Branch image T-351)*

⋁ Another image of 85 Squadron Meteor NF.14s, this time in a formation of four aircraft (consisting of WS782, WS737, WS780 and WS744) flying over the south coast in June 1954. The fastest version of the Meteor to be produced, the NF.14, entered squadron service in early 1954. The aircraft was described by the then Secretary of State for Air, the Lord de l'Isle and Dudley VC, as 'the most effective night fighter that exists'. These were the first photographs to be released of the NF.14 in squadron service and show to great advantage the type's clear-vision canopy for the pilot and observer, and the modified shape of the tail fin. *(Crown Copyright/Air Historical Branch image PRB-1-8271)*

▲ English Electric Canberra PR.7, WH779, pictured on 24 June 1954, shortly after being issued to 542 Squadron at RAF Wyton. 542 Squadron operated the Canberra PR.7 at Wyton from May 1954 until October 1955 when the unit was disbanded. *(Crown Copyright/Air Historical Branch image PRB-1-8322)*

▼ A Hastings Met.1 aircraft (TG616) heads out over the Atlantic on a weather reconnaissance sortie on 9 August 1954. The information radioed back to base was flashed to the Central Forecasting Office at Dunstable and formed the basis of daily weather reports. TG616 was one of a number of Hastings C.1 aircraft converted for this special role. Most, including TG616, were later reverted back to C.1 status. The aircraft served with No 202 Squadron of Coastal Command, based at RAF Aldergrove, from 1953 until the unit was disbanded on 31 July 1964. *(Crown Copyright/Air Historical Branch image PRB-1-8568a)*

Flying Officer Hugh C.H. Merewether, of 615 (County of Surrey) Squadron Royal Auxiliary Air Force, flying his Meteor F.8, WF757, in a vertical climb on 22 August 1954. He was rehearsing an aerobatic display for the forthcoming Battle of Britain 'At Home' display that took take place at RAF Biggin Hill on Saturday, 18 September. Members of the RAuxAF were part-time flyers and the original file note records that 'In his "private life" Flying Officer Merewether is a test pilot for a well-known aircraft concern.' *(Crown Copyright/Air Historical Branch image PRB-1-8610)*

Gloster Meteor F.8s of the two Royal Auxiliary Air Force units based at RAF Biggin Hill – Nos 615 (County of Surrey) Squadron (nearest four aircraft: WH280, WH253, WF757 and WF678) and 600 (City of London) Squadron (consisting of WH759/U, VZ500/R, WH281/Z and WK805/W) – photographed while rehearsing on 22 August 1954 for the station's forthcoming Battle of Britain 'At Home' display. Once again, the file note records the 'part-time' nature of the RAuxAF squadrons by indicating, 'The two squadron commanders, Squadron Leaders R.A. Eeles and J.M. Cormack, lead aircraft piloted by a stockbroker, a hydraulics engineer, a civil servant in the Ministry of Supply, an airline pilot, an employee in the soft drinks industry and a sugar broker.' *(Crown Copyright/Air Historical Branch image PRB-1-8616)*

Over the North Pole

In February 1954, *Aries IV*, a Canberra aircraft from the Royal Air Force Flying College at Manby, made the first flight by a British jet over the Geographical North Pole. The flight routed from Churchill, Alaska, over the North Pole, before returning to Churchill. The flight was piloted by Wing Commander C.S.G. Stanbury and was made during daylight with navigation being checked using the sun. The thermometer at 45,000ft showed -46°F, representing 78 degrees of frost.

Hunter joins 43 Squadron

The first production version of the Hunter F.1 (WT555) made its maiden flight on 16 May 1953. Eventually 113 were built by Hawker at Kingston and a further twenty-six at the Blackpool factory. The need to incorporate the ventral air brake below the fuselage delayed entry of the F.1 into service and it was July 1954 before they were delivered to 43 Squadron at RAF Leuchars. The F.1 remained with 43 Squadron until November 1956 although the F.4 had started to arrive with the squadron in February of the same year.

Swift enters service

The Swift was developed from the earlier Supermarine Type 510 and 535 prototypes of 1948 and 1950. Two prototypes and one hundred production aircraft were ordered in November 1950 as a safeguard against the possible failure of the Hunter, which had been ordered a month earlier. This order was later increased to 150 after the first prototype (WJ960) had flown on 5 August 1951. The Swift F.1, with twin 30mm Aden guns, no reheat and a fixed tailplane, was delivered into service with 56 Squadron at RAF Waterbeach in August 1954. In August of the same year the F.2 variant – with four Aden guns and a cranked leading edge to the wings – was also delivered to 56 Squadron. Both variants remained with the squadron until March 1955 when they were both replaced in service by the Hunter F.5.

SBAC Show highlights

Highlights of the SBAC Show at Farnborough, held from 6–12 September 1954, included the Vickers Varsity VX835, which was powered by a pair of Napier Eland turboprop engines and was subsequently used as a flying

Y VX835 was the second Vickers Varsity aircraft and made its first flight on 29 January 1950. When production of the Varsity finished in February 1954, a total of 160 had been built. The type was eventually withdrawn from service in 1976. VX835 was later fitted with Napier Eland turboprop engines and was photographed around the time of the SBAC Air Show at Farnborough in September 1954. *(Crown Copyright/Air Historical Branch image PRB-1-8666b)*

test-bed for the new engines; two new versions of the Canberra – the B(I).8 and the 'Sapphire-Canberra'; along with the first example of the Folland Midge – a single-seat experimental forerunner of the two-seat Gnat trainer.

The prototype Canberra B.8 (VX185) was converted to the B(I).8 and made its initial post-conversion flight on 23 July 1954. It differed from earlier Canberra aircraft in having an offset fighter-style canopy and accommodation for the navigator/bomb-aimer in the redesigned nose. A gun pack with four 30mm guns could also be fitted beneath the fuselage.

The 'Sapphire-Canberra' was a standard B.2 (WD933) used by Armstrong Siddeley for development tests with their Sapphire Sa6/7 turbojet engines.

The Folland Midge was powered by an Armstrong Siddeley Viper turbojet engine, and, carrying the markings G-39-1, made its first flight on 11 August 1954, barely a month before appearing at the SBAC Show.

➤ **The Fairey FD.1 research aircraft, VX350, was the first British-built delta-winged aircraft and the smallest aircraft on display at the SBAC Show at Farnborough in 1954. The aircraft was originally conceived as a vertical take-off fighter, intended to be launched from an inclined ramp. Already in the early design stage at Fairey, the Ministry of Supply (MoS) decided to have the aircraft built as a more conventional jet-powered research vehicle to specification E.10/47. With a wingspan of 19ft 6in and just 26ft long, the Rolls-Royce Derwent-powered aircraft was designed to investigate the handling characteristics of delta-wing aircraft at transonic speeds. In testing, however, it was found that the aircraft suffered from stability problems which, even after a series of modifications following a landing accident in September 1951, could not be fully cured. With limited flying after the test programme was relaunched in May 1953, and no sign of a resolution of the considerable design deficiencies, the FD.1 was soon relegated to non-flying status and ended its life on the range at Shoeburyness. Only one FD.1 was built, with the second (VX357) and third (VX364) airframes being cancelled before they entered production.** *(Crown Copyright/Air Historical Branch image PRB-1-8667)*

➤ The Folland Midge was a single-seat experimental forerunner of the two-seat Gnat trainer. The Midge was powered by an Armstrong Siddeley Viper turbojet engine, while the Gnat used the new 4,230lb-thrust Bristol Orpheus engine. The Midge (carrying the markings G-39-1) made its first flight on 11 August 1954, barely a month before this photograph was taken during the SBAC Air Show at Farnborough in September 1954. *(Crown Copyright/ Air Historical Branch image PRB-1-8668)*

◄ A new version of the Canberra was debuted at the SBAC Air Show at Farnborough in September 1954. The prototype B.8 Canberra, VX185, was converted to the B(I).8 and made its initial post-conversion flight on 23 July 1954. It differed from earlier Canberra aircraft in having an offset fighter-style canopy and accommodation for the navigator/bomb-aimer in the redesigned nose. A gun pack with four 30mm guns could also be fitted beneath the fuselage. The first of eighty production B(I).8s (WT326) made its first flight on 8 June 1955 and the type first entered service with No 88 Squadron in Germany in January 1956. *(Crown Copyright/Air Historical Branch image PRB-1-8669b)*

⋀ The 'Sapphire-Canberra', a standard B.2, WD933, used by Armstrong Siddeley for development tests with their Sapphire Sa6/7 turbojet engines. The aircraft was displayed at the SBAC Show at Farnborough in September 1954 when this photograph was taken. *(Crown Copyright/Air Historical Branch image PRB-1-8675)*

⋁ Two Meteor F.8s (unidentified but coded 'T' and 'Y') of the Day Fighter Leader's School – part of the Central Fighter Establishment at RAF West Raynham – are seen here while taking off for a training flight in December 1954. *(Crown Copyright/ Air Historical Branch image PRB-1-8813)*

Canberra T.4s, flown by instructors from 231 Operational Conversion Unit at RAF Bassingbourn, are seen here in formation during a training flight in November 1954. The T.4 was a dual-control version of the Canberra with side-by-side seating. The aircraft here are WE195, WH841, WH843 and WH844. *(Above: Crown Copyright/Air Historical Branch image PRB-1-8963; below: Crown Copyright/Air Historical Branch image PRB-1-8970)*

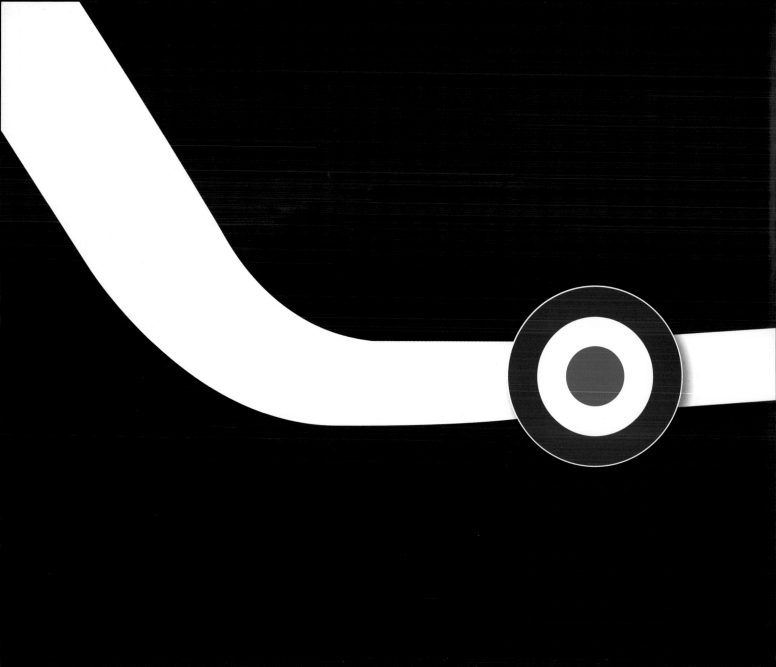

1955

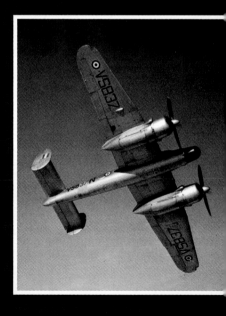

Delivery of atomic weapons to the RAF had already begun, and, in January 1955, the first aircraft capable of carrying them – the Vickers Valiant – was introduced into service with 138 Squadron at RAF Gaydon. The government of the day recognised that if such weapons were ever used in war, they would cause destruction at an unprecedented level – on both humans and infrastructure. It would result in a struggle for survival, the catastrophic results of which were impossible to foresee with any degree of accuracy. The UK Government decided it was essential that such facts ought to be known – not just by UK citizens, but the entire world. All should recognise the magnitude of destruction that a nuclear war would cause, in the hope that it would generate a compelling will for peace strong enough to influence even the most dictatorial rulers. Possessing a nuclear capability should provide a deterrent to others, making it a weapon of hope rather than despair.

In 1955, the free world had a marked superiority both in nuclear weapons themselves as well as in the means to deliver them. The UK Government considered that such a powerful deterrent had significantly reduced the risk of major war. Unfortunately, the bulk of that deterrent was in the hands of the US Government and their Strategic Air Command (SAC). As a consequence, on 7 February the UK Government took the decision to increase its own deterrent by building up its stock of nuclear weapons, as well as increasing their ability to deliver them. If, despite the deterrent, it were ever to come to global war, it was recognised that in the crucial initial phase, the primary role would fall to the RAF. With that in mind, the allocation of Air Ministry funds was increased, both to build up the strategic bomber force as well as to provide a modernised UK defence system including an improved control and reporting capability, all-weather radar-equipped fighters and air-to-air and ground-to-air guided weapons.

⋀ This unique photograph, taken in August 1955, shows a mixed aerobatic formation comprising aircraft and pilots of leading aerobatic teams of the RAF, Royal Canadian Air Force and United States Air Force based in Europe. At the head of the quartet is Hunter F.1, WW636, of 54 Squadron based at RAF Odiham, flown by Captain Richard G. Imming, a USAF officer serving with the RAF on an exchange posting. On either side of him are two Sabres of the Sky Lancers team from No 2 Wing RCAF based at Grostenquin, France. In the slot position is a Lockheed T-33 Shooting Star trainer from the Aerojets team of No 7330 Flying Training Wing, Fürstenfeldbruck, Germany. This formation, which was apparently unrehearsed, was flown when the three teams were appearing at an airshow in Metz, France. *(Crown Copyright/Air Historical Branch image PRB-1-10227)*

North American Sabre F.4, XB748/F, of 234 Squadron based at Geilenkirchen, Germany, photographed in flight in January 1955. The Sabre was the first swept-wing fighter used by the RAF and served mainly with 2nd Tactical Air Force fighter squadrons based in Germany as a stop-gap measure until the arrival of the Hawker Hunter jet fighters with 2TAF squadrons in 1955. Some 430 Sabres served with the RAF, all built under licence by Canadair in Canada and flown across the North Atlantic between December 1952 and May 1954 in Operation Becher's Brook. *(Crown Copyright/Air Historical Branch image PRB-1-9231)*

North American Sabre F.4s (XB867/E, XB885/D and one unidentified) of 234 Squadron based at Geilenkirchen, Germany, photographed in flight in January 1955. *(Crown Copyright/Air Historical Branch image PRB-1-9232)*

All-jet training

With increasing numbers of jet aircraft entering service with the RAF, more interest was shown by Parliament in RAF training methods and costs, as well as in accidents to jet aircraft. Methods then in use with pilot training – operating with No 5 Flying Training School at Oakington – involved the use of the Piston Provost and Vampire aircraft as training platforms. The scheme successfully removed unsuitable trainees from the process before they obtained their wings, although it was reported in Parliament by George Ward, Under Secretary of State for Air, that 'it was now costing £25,000 to put a single pilot into a bomber squadron'. Mr Ward defended the piston-engined Provost/Vampire jet training sequence in the House of Commons, and added that the introduction as an experiment of a jet aircraft to replace the Piston Provost for *basic* jet training was being considered. He went on to emphasise that the fatality rate in jet accidents during 1953 had been roughly half of the lowest fatal accident rate for the Spitfire when in comparable service.

In August 1955, the all-jet training programme referred to by George Ward was launched on an experimental basis with No 2 Flying Training School at RAF Hullavington with the Jet Provost T.1. Two courses ran side-by-side; the first used the Piston Provost, while the second – the new all-jet scheme – used the Jet Provost for basic jet training. On 17 October 1955, the first student to fly solo on a jet aircraft without any previous piston-engined flying experience (Pilot Officer R.T. Foster) did so after just 8 hours and 20 minutes of dual instruction on the Jet Provost T.1.

Manpower shortages

At the beginning of 1955, a shortage of skilled men in the RAF was a cause for considerable concern among senior officers and politicians. This, along with the increasing complexity of the new jet-powered aircraft, was making things difficult – especially at squadron level. Most RAF stations were undermanned in the advanced trades and this resulted in excessive demands on those men who were available. Advanced tradesmen, who were far short of the agreed requirement, could not supervise properly because they themselves had to do much of the work that ought to have been completely by less skilled and qualified individuals. Despite this situation, most RAF stations were getting the work completed by overworking their few skilled advanced tradesmen and by improvisation. Yet many stations had a greater number of men than theoretically required; this was often in an attempt to compensate for

the lack of appropriate skilled individuals by having a surplus of mechanics or by misemploying other types of advanced tradesmen. Both these courses of action were wasteful.

A Parliamentary Committee on Estimates considered the situation and decided that a greater saving in the demands of the highly skilled craftsmen could be achieved if instrument and sub-assemblies were returned to the manufacturer for repair or overhaul. It was accepted that such a system would require significant increases in the inventory of spare parts, but this was considered to be an acceptable price to pay.

At the same time, the committee reported details of a contract granted to Flight Refuelling Limited, to operate a jet training school at Tarrant Rushton. Service instructors gave tuition in aircraft serviced by civilians. The Air Ministry estimated that the work handled by 145 civilians would have required around 350 servicemen. It was a sign of things to come!

Civilianising military operations would not cure all the problems of RAF staffing levels. There was still the problem of a significant shortage of highly skilled technical grades – roles usually filled by volunteers on long-term Regular engagements. The situation at the time was that about 75 per cent of the ground staff were on engagements of five years, of which over 50 per cent were on National Service or on three-year engagements. One consequence was that, whereas a training course need only be provided once if a trainee was intending to serve for twenty years, it had to be provided four times to men engaging for five years and ten times to National Servicemen.

The committee considered that the principal deterrents to regular engagements were bad accommodation (particularly married quarters), difficulties over children's education, and what was known as 'turbulence' – the unceasing movement of officers and men from station to station. In the six months to 30 April 1954, 13.4 per cent of the trained regular ground airmen moved from one place to another; overseas postings accounted for another 10.7 per cent, while the loss to civilian life a further 19.8 per cent. The report concluded that nearly half of the trained regular ground staff moved in the course of one year!

The arrival of increasing numbers of new jet-engined aircraft into squadrons compounded the manning problems and made the discovery of a solution increasingly urgent. By the middle of 1955, more than 375 British aircraft – consisting of Canberra, Valiant and Hunter aircraft – had been delivered to the RAF and, perhaps more importantly, paid for with the help of American 'offshore' purchase arrangements.

The Whirlwind enters service

The Whirlwind helicopter was the Westland-built military version of the Sikorsky S-55 for service with the RAF and the Royal Navy. The first Whirlwind HAR.1 (XA862) made its maiden flight on 15 August 1953 and was later delivered to the Royal Navy. The first variant for the RAF was the HAR.2 which began deliveries in 1955. The HAR.2 was powered by a Pratt & Whitney R-1340-40 engine producing 600hp, and around sixty were produced for both communications as well as search and rescue (SAR) duties with Transport and Coastal Commands. The first deliveries of the HAR.2 were made to 22 Squadron, Coastal Command, at Thorney Island in February 1955, soon after the unit had reformed as a post-war SAR unit. Here, they operated alongside Sycamore HC.12 helicopters for around six months.

The Whirlwind HAR.2s operated in the now-familiar all-yellow finish when serving as part of the UK's SAR Organisation, and played a pioneering role in the build-up of the SAR helicopter fleet. While based at Thorney Island, 22 Squadron provided a SAR detachment of HAR.2 helicopters to RAF Valley, Felixstowe and Martlesham Heath. In June 1956, 22 Squadron moved to RAF St Mawgan, and while resident here, provided SAR detachments to Chivenor, Felixstowe, Tangmere, Thorney Island, Valley, Manston and Coltishall. The HAR.2s remained in service with 22 Squadron until replaced by the HAR.10 version in August 1962.

◁ Westland Whirlwind HAR.2, XJ429, photographed in January 1955 while in use with the A&AEE. XJ429 had originally been allocated a serial number within the 'compromised' batch XD777-784, but was subsequently renumbered. XJ429 was later converted to HAR.10 status. The Whirlwind HAR.2 entered service with 22 Squadron, Coastal Command, at Thorney Island in February 1955. *(Crown Copyright/Air Historical Branch image PRB-1-9290)*

➤ Prior to the introduction of a dedicated winch man and the bosun's chair for search and rescue purposes, helicopters were required to hover just feet above the water and lift survivors aboard in a contraption known as a 'Sproule net' (also known as 'wet winching'). This method required the helicopter to be precisely positioned and the survivor to climb into the net unaided, a feat which could end with the helicopter ditching due to the unreliable and underpowered engines of early Whirlwinds. This picture of XJ430 (an early Whirlwind HAR.2) demonstrating the skill, was taken in June 1955. *(Crown Copyright/Air Historical Branch image PRB-1-9913)*

Bristol Brigand T.5, VS837/N, one of a number used by 238 Operational Conversion Unit at RAF Colerne for aircrew training, photographed in flight on 8 March 1955. The OCU was formed in June 1952 following the renaming of the Air Interception School and was tasked with the training of night fighter radar operators in the tracking methods required at night and in poor weather using either the unit's Brigand or Balliol aircraft as targets. *(Above: Crown Copyright/Air Historical Branch image PRB-1-9411; left: Crown Copyright/Air Historical Branch image PRB-1-9412)*

Ⅴ Bristol Brigand T.5, VS837/N, of 238 Operational Conversion Unit at RAF Colerne in company with Gloster Meteor NF.14, WS752, of 85 Squadron during a training sortie on 8 March 1955. Note that the black hood in the rear cockpit of the Brigand has been unfolded to simulate night conditions for the student air intercept radar operator. Brigands operated with the RAF until March 1958 when 238 OCU, then based at RAF North Luffenham, was disbanded. *(Crown Copyright/Air Historical Branch image PRB-1-9413)*

Overseas operations

In 1955, Britain was involved in emergencies in Malaya, Kenya, Oman and Cyprus. After having had a long-term interest in Egypt and, in particular, the Suez Canal, Britain was withdrawing its troops from the region while still maintaining stocks in key strategic locations for defence activities, should they ever be required. Britain had an agreement for the use and defence of the Canal Zone from Egypt's President Nasser.

During 1955, the wind of change was blowing with increasing strength outside Europe, yet the UK was responsible for maintaining order in many parts of the world. To assist in this, the RAF was required to maintain forces in the Middle and Far East. On 7 July 1955, the Air Forces in the Middle East were reorganised into two groups. The Northern Group was under Air Headquarters Levant, in Nicosia, to control assets in Iraq, Jordan, Libya and Cyprus. The Southern Group was under Headquarters British Forces in Aden, responsible for units in the Aden Protectorate, along the South Arabian coast, in the Persian Gulf and also in Kenya; as well as the en route staging posts.

In March 1955, operations in Malaya continued at a pace. Squadron Leader N.P.W. Hancock, the Commanding Officer of 33 Squadron, led a flight of Hornet F.3s on their 5,000th operational sortie against communist nationalists. The Hornet F.3 was the last piston-engined aircraft in service with any RAF front-line squadron and provided sterling service in Malaya – despite their wooden construction – where they provided rocket-strike attack capabilities against the communist forces. They were eventually replaced in theatre by the Vampire FB.9.

Although not part of operations against the EOKA terrorists in Cyprus, a number of Canberra B.2 aircraft from 21 and 27 Squadrons visited the island and were temporarily based at Nicosia. Aircraft from both squadrons were undertaking a planned visit to RAF bases in the Mediterranean and Middle East from their base at RAF Scampton in 1955.

Canberra B.2 aircraft of Nos 21 and 27 Squadrons (including WH729) being serviced on the flight line at Nicosia, Cyprus. The aircraft from these squadrons were undertaking a visit to RAF bases in the Mediterranean and Middle East from their home base at RAF Scampton, 1955. *(Above: Crown Copyright/Air Historical Branch image CMP-708; below: Crown Copyright/Air Historical Branch image CMP-709)*

Four Canberra B.2 aircraft (WJ609, WJ722, WJ977 and WJ715) of 21 Squadron fly past the black, rugged mountains of Aden, during a visit to bases of the Middle East Air Force from their base at RAF Scampton, 1955. *(Above: Crown Copyright/Air Historical Branch image CMP-743; below: Crown Copyright/Air Historical Branch image CMP-744)*

In March 1955, Squadron Leader N.P.W. Hancock, the Commanding Officer of 33 Squadron, led a flight of Hornet F.3 aircraft on their 5,000th operational sortie against communist nationalists in Malaya. The squadron leader is pictured in the cockpit of his aircraft just prior to take-off. *(Crown Copyright/Air Historical Branch image CFP-855)*

Four Hunter F.2s (WN950/F, WN915/I, WN948/R and WN952/G) of 257 Squadron based at RAF Wattisham, photographed in formation on 14 April 1955. The F.2, of which only forty-five were built, served only with Nos 257 and 263 Squadrons, between September 1954 and March 1957. Like the earlier Hunter F.1, the aircraft suffered from a lack of range and was soon superseded by the improved F.4, deliveries of which started in June 1955 to Fighter Command squadrons. *(Crown Copyright/Air Historical Branch image PRB-1-9505)*

Gloster Meteor F.8, WK935, was modified to accommodate a second pilot in the prone position for trials with the Institute of Aviation Medicine at Farnborough and was photographed during a test flight on 2 May 1955. The second pilot rested on a rubber couch with arm and chin rests and controlled the aircraft using a side-stick and hanging pedals operated by moving his ankles. To counterbalance this extra length and weight, WK935 was fitted with the tail section from an NF.12 and the flying controls were power-boosted. A total of ninety-nine flights were carried out before the project was ended and the aircraft was placed in store in April 1956. It was subsequently preserved at the RAF Museum's Cosford site. *(Crown Copyright/Air Historical Branch image PRB-1-9574)*

A view of Squadron Leader R.S. Wambeek, a flying doctor with the Institute of Aviation Medicine at Farnborough, demonstrating the pilot in the prone position of WK935 (see photograph above). Not obvious from this picture are the ankle-operated pedals used to control the Meteor's flying control surfaces. *(Crown Copyright/Air Historical Branch image PRB-1-9578)*

⋀ Groundcrew of the Flying Boat Training Squadron launch one of their Sunderland GR.5s, SZ560/D, on the slipway at Pembroke Dock in June 1955. *(Crown Copyright/Air Historical Branch image PRB-1-9773)*

⋁ Three Canberra B.6 aircraft of 101 Squadron (WJ756, WJ758 and WJ762) were detached from RAF Binbrook in June 1955 to Changi, Singapore, for a series of flying and systems trials for the aircraft under tropical conditions. During the type's first operational visit to the region, the Canberra aircraft were also used to bomb nationalist targets in Malaya as part of Operation Firedog. *(Crown Copyright/Air Historical Branch image CFP-874)*

⋀ Hastings C.4, WJ324, was one of four specially configured aircraft used by the VIP Flight of 24 Squadron based at RAF Abingdon. It was photographed on 30 June 1955. *(Crown Copyright/Air Historical Branch image PRB-1-10060)*

➤ Two Jet Provost T.1s, XD676 and XD677, flying over The Needles during a test sortie on 28 June 1955 when both aircraft were based at Boscombe Down with the Aeroplane and Armament Experimental Establishment (A&AEE). Both aircraft – part of the RAF's first batch of ten aircraft (serial numbers XD674-680, 692-693) – had recently arrived at the A&AEE to undertake pre-service trials before being issued to the Central Flying School at RAF Little Rissington where they were used to validate the concept of an all-jet training syllabus for future pilots. *(Crown Copyright/Air Historical Branch image PRB-1-10082)*

◄ Hunter F.1s, WT659, WT687, WW610 and WW641, of 54 Squadron, rehearsing on 14 July 1955 for their forthcoming appearance at the Metz International Air Display on 31 July. The Odiham-based squadron only flew the F.1 for six months (between April and September 1955) before re-equipping with the Hunter F.4 variant. The F.1 aircraft were passed to 229 Operational Conversion Unit and 43 Squadron (WW641). *(Crown Copyright/Air Historical Branch image PRB-1-10125)*

➤ The Commanding Officer of 24 Squadron, Squadron Leader D.P. Boulnois, explains to HRH the Duke of Edinburgh how a Hastings can be used to drop supplies utilising externally mounted parachute containers, during a visit to RAF Abingdon on 22 July 1955. Looking on are the station commander, Group Captain Haggar and Air-Vice Marshal Beamish. *(Crown Copyright/Air Historical Branch image PRB-1-10194)*

⋀ Bristol Sycamore HR.14, XG501, of 275 Squadron, based at RAF Thornaby, takes off after participating in a search and rescue demonstration at Flamborough Head on 4 August 1955. XG501 joined the squadron in April 1955 but was written off on 15 December 1955 when the tail rotor struck a mast on Bell Rock Lighthouse and it fell onto the rocks below. *(Crown Copyright/Air Historical Branch image PRB-1-10246)*

⋁ The first air-to-air pictures of the Hunter F.5 were issued in August 1955. These aircraft, from 41 Squadron based at Biggin Hill, were pictured as they rehearsed for the station's forthcoming Battle of Britain air display on 17 September.
(Crown Copyright/Air Historical Branch image PRB-1-10337)

Highlights of the SBAC Show

The SBAC Show held at Farnborough from 5–11 September 1955 was another classic event. Massive crowds flocked to the show and were rewarded with a large selection of aircraft, many of them making their first appearances at the event. These included the Avro Shackleton MR.3, Hawker Hunter T.7 and the Bristol Type 173 twin-rotor helicopter.

Also making an appearance was Hunter F.4 (WV385) carrying the latest 100-gallon asbestos under-wing drop-tanks. XA890, the second production-standard Vulcan B.1, appeared while still fitted with the original wing with straight leading edges. XA890 had the revised nose containing the aircraft's H2S navigation radar and was painted in the striking silver colour scheme applied to early Vulcan aircraft, before the application of all-over white 'anti-flash' paint.

The first Avro Shackleton MR.3, WR970, featured a revised cockpit, various internal improvements (including a liberal amount of soundproofing), additional wing-tip fuel tanks and tricycle undercarriage. Sadly, WR970

was lost in tragic circumstances during stall tests on 7 December 1956.

The first prototype Hunter T.7 two-seat side-by-side trainer, WJ615, appeared at the show only two months after its maiden flight. This aircraft differed from all other T.7s built, having a cockpit canopy which was less humped than subsequent aircraft as it generated unacceptable airflow instability.

The Bristol Type 173 Mk 2 twin-rotor helicopter, XH379, made an appearance at the 1955 SBAC Show. The prototype Mk 1 G-ALBN had made its first flight back on 3 January 1953; unfortunately, it preferred to fly backwards – until modifications corrected the issue. The Type 173 Mk 2 was initially considered for possible use in the anti-submarine role, but after further development as the Type 192 it eventually entered service with the RAF as the Belvedere HC.1 and served between 1961 and 1969 – becoming the first twin-engined, twin-rotor helicopter to operate with the RAF.

▼ **Hawker Hunter F.4, WV385, carrying the latest 100-gallon asbestos under-wing drop-tanks, photographed in September 1955.**
(Crown Copyright/Air Historical Branch image PRB-1-10343)

◄ XA890, the second production-standard Vulcan B.1, is pictured here during its appearance at the SBAC Air Show at Farnborough in September 1955. While still fitted with the original wing with straight leading edges, XA890 had the revised nose containing the aircraft's H2S navigation radar. *(Crown Copyright/Air Historical Branch image PRB-1-10352)*

➤ The first Avro Shackleton MR.3, WR970, pictured at the time of its debut at the SBAC Air Show at Farnborough in September 1955. *(Crown Copyright/Air Historical Branch image PRB-1-10356)*

◄ The first prototype Hunter T.7 two-seat side-by-side trainer, WJ615, pictured in September 1955, two months after its maiden flight. This aircraft differed from all other T.7s built, having a cockpit canopy which was less humped than subsequent aircraft as it generated unacceptable airflow instability. A total of forty-seven were built for the RAF and the first entered service with 229 Operational Conversion Unit at RAF Chivenor in August 1958. Several of the type also participated in the 1959 London–Paris Air Race (see also page 275, top). The last Hunters in RAF service were those used by the Buccaneer squadrons at RAF Lossiemouth as conversion trainers until April 1994. *(Crown Copyright/Air Historical Branch image PRB-1-10357)*

➤ Bristol Type 173 twin-rotor helicopter, XH379, displaying at the SBAC Air Show at Farnborough in September 1955. Its modified successor, the Belvedere HC.1, became the first twin-engined, twin-rotor helicopter to serve with the **RAF**. *(Crown Copyright/Air Historical Branch image PRB-1-10373)*

∨ A manufacturer's photograph of a Shackleton MR.2 carrying a 31ft Saro Mk.3 motor-driven airborne lifeboat in the bomb bay. Once dropped, the lifeboat's descent was checked by four parachutes which automatically released from the boat upon contact with water. It was capable of holding ten people with rations for up to fourteen days. This system was later dropped in favour of 'Lindholme Gear' (also known as Air-Sea Rescue Apparatus Mk.4) with floating ropes, an inflatable nine-man life raft and stores containers. Note the two remotely operated guns which were controlled from the crew position in the nose. *(Crown Copyright/Air Historical Branch image PRB-1-10732)*

The four Hawker Hunter F.4s of the 43 Squadron aerobatic team – WT582/B, WT618/D, WT622/G and WW645/S – break from echelon formation during a practice flight on 10 October 1955. *(Crown Copyright/Air Historical Branch image PRB-1-10614)*

Meteor NF.14, WS848, of the Fighter Command Communications Squadron at RAF Bovingdon. WS848 was the very last Meteor to be built. Completed in May 1954, the aircraft remained with Armstrong Whitworth for a twelve-month period before joining the Central Fighter Establishment at RAF West Raynham. In October 1955, WS848 was transferred to the FCCS where it remained until withdrawn from use in October 1962 and was scrapped a year later. *(Crown Copyright/Air Historical Branch image PRB-1-10984)*

21st anniversary of in-flight refuelling

What had begun in 1935 as an almost casual experiment by Sir Alan Cobham – perhaps Britain's greatest long-distance airman – had by 1955 reached a point in its development where air forces of the world, including the RAF, had placed significant orders for the 'drogue and probe' in-flight refuelling equipment. This equipment would play a significant part in future RAF activities when one Middle East country after another closed its airspace to overflying RAF aircraft.

Farewell to the Mosquito PR.34

On 15 December 1955, when 81 Squadron Mosquito PR34, RG314, took off from its base at Seletar, Singapore, it was flying the very last operational mission by the type. The two-man crew of RG314 on this historic occasion were Flying Officer Alexander J. Knox and his navigator, Flying Officer Arnold B. Thompson. The Mosquito PR.34 had joined 81 Squadron in September 1946 and had seen significant service in the Far East. While 81 Squadron operated a variety of photo-reconnaissance assets, the Mosquito PR.34 was effectively replaced by the Meteor PR.10.

De Havilland Mosquito PR.34, RG314, of 81 Squadron. This aircraft, which flew the final operational mission for the type in RAF service on 15 December 1955, is pictured over its base at Seletar, Singapore. The Mosquito PR.34 had joined 81 Squadron in September 1946 and had seen significant service in the Far East. While 81 Squadron operated a variety of photo-reconnaissance assets, the Mosquito PR.34 was effectively replaced by the Meteor PR.10. *(Crown Copyright/Air Historical Branch image CFP-921)*

The two-man crew of de Havilland Mosquito PR.34, RG314, of 81 Squadron which flew the final operational mission for the type in RAF service on 15 December 1955. They are Flying Officer Alexander J. Knox (right) and his navigator, Flying Officer Arnold B. Thompson (left). *(Crown Copyright/Air Historical Branch image CFP-922)*

⚠ Three Hawker Hunter F.1s (WT594/U, WT622/G and WT641/T) of the 43 Squadron aerobatic team The Fighting Cocks, are seen here looping their aircraft in formation, close to their base at RAF Leuchars in 1955. The squadron was the first to be equipped with the Hunter, receiving their first aircraft in the summer of 1954. The squadron's Commanding Officer, Squadron Leader R.E. Le Long, led the three-ship team and picked two Sergeant Pilots, Tom Lampitt and Norman Lamb, as his wing men. Their first display was at Ypenburg, Holland, on 30 May 1955, and they rapidly gained a reputation as one of the very best aerobatic teams of the day. Following the departure of Squadron Leader Le Long in the summer of 1955, two new pilots, Flight Lieutenant Pete Bairsto and Flying Officer Ron Smith, were added to create a four-ship routine in time for the Battle of Britain displays at Turnhouse and Leuchars in September – the latter being preceded by a low pass along Princes Street in Edinburgh! *(Crown Copyright/Air Historical Branch image T-42a)*

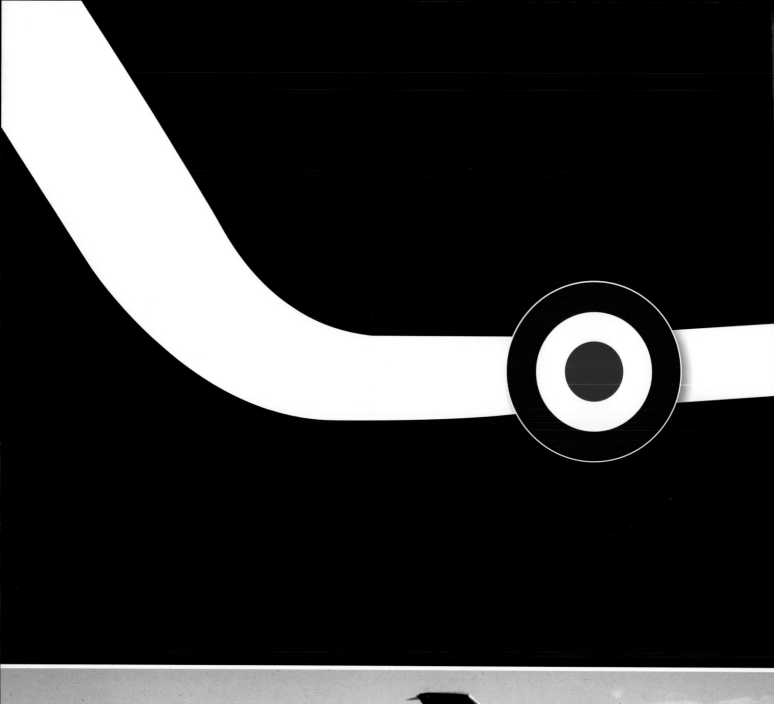

1956

The Suez Crisis

In October 1954, Egypt abrogated the treaty whereby the British Army and the RAF were permitted bases in the Canal Zone until 1956, with the possibility of extension beyond that date by negotiation. Withdrawals began to bases in Cyprus and Aden, which were to become the major centres of the British military presence in the Middle East. In the summer of 1956, just three months after the British withdrawal had been completed, a major crisis broke.

On 26 July 1956, President Nasser of Egypt announced the nationalisation of the Suez Canal Company. This was in retaliation for the British and US Governments reneging on an agreement for the financing of the Aswan Dam project. The Suez Canal represented the main source of the supply of oil for both Britain and France, and the potential loss of those supplies represented an economic threat that they could not ignore. In addition, there was a significant increase in military aid for Egypt from the Communist Bloc.

The following day, the British Prime Minister – Sir Anthony Eden – formed the 'Egypt Committee', consisting of himself, Lord Salisbury (Leader of the House of Lords), Lord Holme (Commonwealth Secretary) and Harold Macmillan (Chancellor of the Exchequer), to coordinate Britain's intent to recover her access to the Suez Canal. Selwyn Lloyd (Foreign Secretary) and Sir Walter Monckton (Defence Minster) were later added to the 'Egypt Committee'.

A A line of Gloster Javelin F(AW).1s of 46 Squadron on the flightline at Odiham in 1956. Identifiable aircraft include XA619/O, XA620/E and XA569/A. The Javelin F(AW).1 had entered service in February 1956 and 46 Squadron were the first recipients of the type when a batch of aircraft was delivered in that month. *(Crown Copyright/Air Historical Branch image T-302)*

On 11 August, on his appointment as Commander-in-Chief British Middle East Land Forces, General Sir Charles E. Keightley was informed, that in view of Egypt's action, the British and French Governments had decided to concentrate certain forces in the Eastern Mediterranean in readiness for an armed intervention should it become necessary to protect their interests. Certain naval, land and air forces were earmarked and alerted, while a small Allied Headquarters was set up in London to prepare contingency plans.

In the middle of August, a conference of nations was held in London in an attempt to find a diplomatic solution. It adopted eighteen proposals which included an offer to Nasser of Egyptian representation on the Suez Company board and a share in its profits. At the beginning of September, the Australian Prime Minister, Sir Robert Menzies, travelled to Cairo to offer Nasser the eighteen proposals – which he rejected. Meanwhile, the US Secretary of State, John Foster Dulles, sought to distance the US Government from supporting a military intervention, ever-mindful of President Eisenhower's hopes for re-election in the November US Presidential Election.

It was soon recognised by UK military planners that one of the main limitations to prospective operations would be the shortage of airfields in Cyprus. Initially, only one airfield – at Nicosia – was available, but two further airfields, at Akrotiri and Tymbou, were quickly developed during September and October.

A second conference of nations was held in London from 19–21 September to discuss American proposals for a Suez Canal Users Association, to ensure continued international use of the canal. Unfortunately, the USSR vetoed the American plan in the United Nations Security Council on 13 October.

The following day, Sir Anthony Eden held secret discussions with French officials over a military operation to recover use of the Suez Canal. The talks resulted in the formation of a plan by which Israel would invade Egypt and thus allow British and French forces to seize the canal as an act of intervention between warring nations.

Towards the end of October, Selwyn Lloyd, the British Foreign Secretary, concluded an agreement with France and Israeli officials at Sèvres, France. The British copy of the resulting Sèvres Protocol was subsequently destroyed on the orders of Sir Anthony Eden. On 25 October, Eden gained approval for military intervention from a divided Cabinet. An increasingly sidelined Foreign Office was split over the government's intention to adopt military measures.

During the last week of October, intelligence sources were reporting from Tel Aviv and elsewhere on strong

A Bomber Command Valiant B.1 at RAF Luqa for Operation Musketeer. Nos 138, 148 and 207 Squadrons all provided Valiant B.1s at Luqa in the heavy bombing role. When the ceasefire was declared, all three Valiant squadrons left Malta on 7 November 1956 to return to their home bases. *(Crown Copyright/Air Historical Branch image CMP-829)*

indications of Israeli mobilisations, and on 29 October, Israel attacked across the Sinai Peninsula. The following day, the British and French Governments issued an ultimatum to both Israel and Egypt to cease hostilities within 24 hours, to withdraw contestant troops ten miles from the Suez Canal and to allow occupation by Anglo-French forces of Port Said, Ismailia and Suez. At 04.30 the next day, General Keightley was informed that the Israeli Government had agreed to the ultimatum but that Egypt had refused. As Allied Commander, he was required to interpose his forces between those of Israel and Egypt in order to bring a cessation of hostilities and to occupy the three towns.

Operation Musketeer

The Anglo-French seaborne invasion to occupy the Canal Zone, supported by parachute forces, was launched from Malta and Cyprus under the name Operation Musketeer. The RAF was to play a significant role in the mission.

At the time, it was estimated that the Egyptian Air Force had eighty Russian MiG-15 fighters, forty-five Il-28 bombers, twenty-five British-built Meteors and fifty-seven Vampire jets, together with around 200 transport and training aircraft. General Keightley's first priority was to neutralise the threat of the Egyptian Air Force against landing craft conveying commando and armoured forces from Malta, and air transport aircraft flying paratroops from Cyprus. Action by Egyptian Il-28 bombers against overcrowded airfields in Cyprus would have done damage out of all proportion to the effort involved!

The Royal Air Force was well prepared for the action to come. At 16.15 GMT on 31 October, RAF Valiant aircraft of 148 Squadron and Canberra B.2 aircraft from 10 Squadron, along with Canberra B.6 aircraft from 12 Squadron, began their attacks on the Egyptian airfields of Cairo West, Almaza, Bilbeis and Inches from 49,000ft. The attacks were continued through the early part of the night with the aid of flares and encountered a certain amount of anti-aircraft fire, but no night fighters. Air reconnaissance showed that, aside from around ten Il-28 bombers which had been flown out of the target areas, the majority of the Egyptian Air Force combat aircraft had been destroyed or damaged on the ground. Only one RAF aircraft had been attacked in the air and suffered only slight damage, while others incurred minor damage from anti-aircraft fire. Later, when further

reconnaissance was conducted, the Egyptians were attempting to blockade the Suez Canal and ships were seen scuppered across the entrance to Port Said.

By the end of 2 November, it was evident that the task of neutralising the Egyptian Air Force was all but complete. A small number of Il-28 bombers remained untouched at Luxor airfield and these were attacked during the night of 2/3 November and again on 4 November. During 3 November the bulk of the air effort was switched from military airfields to other military targets – mainly to heavy movements in the Canal Zone. Armed reconnaissance sorties found large quantities of military transport activity and considerable numbers of Russian tanks.

On the night of 5/6 November, British and French troops invaded Port Said and took control of the Suez Canal. Nine transport aircraft were hit but all returned safely to base, while Egyptian anti-aircraft fire was dealt with by fighter aircraft operating anti-flak patrols. In a meeting of the British Cabinet later that day, Harold Macmillan raised stark warnings of economic peril as a result of the action, even though he had previously been one of the strongest supporters of resolute action. The US Presidential Elections resulted in the re-election of President Eisenhower. The seaborne assault was equally successful on the following day, supported by naval gunfire and an airstrike.

On 7 November, the United States, USSR and the United Nations condemned the British and French military action. The loss of confidence and American backing for the already weak British economy forced Sir Anthony Eden into calling a ceasefire that meant United Nations troops taking over from British and French troops when the ceasefire became effective at 23.59 hours GMT on 6 November.

The RAF's own casualties were fortunately limited to three officers and one airman killed; no wounded and none missing. Two aircraft had been lost: Canberra PR.7 WH799 of 58 Squadron was shot down off the coast of Syria by a MiG-17, having photographed a cut oil pipeline in Syria; and Canberra B.6 WT371 of 139 Squadron crashed on landing at Nicosia, killing the crew of three, after having been shot up over Port Said.

On 7 November, 138 Squadron returned home to the UK with their Valiant bombers while 10 Squadron Canberra aircraft returned on 9 November. Most units were home by Christmas, but at least three – 15, 61 and 109 Squadrons – did not return until the New Year.

⋀ Bomber Command Canberra aircraft lined up at RAF Luqa, Malta, in readiness for Operation Musketeer. The first two
Canberras on the right of the picture – WH948 and WJ762 – are both B.6 variants. Canberra B.6s from Nos 9, 12, 101, 109 and
139 Squadrons were employed at RAF Luqa during the conflict. *(Crown Copyright/Air Historical Branch image CMP-843)*

⋁ Bomber Command Canberra aircraft on the ramp at RAF Luqa, Malta, for Operation Musketeer. WH967, a B.6 variant from 12
Squadron, can be seen underneath the wing. The special black and yellow recognition stripes seen on WH967 varied from
type to type, and from squadron to squadron. The original order was for two black on three yellow stripes on the rear fuselage
and each wing outboard of the engines. The stripes were to have been 1ft wide on the smaller aircraft and 2ft wide on the
bombers and transport aircraft. Helicopters did not carry the stripes, and neither did the Valiant aircraft. In practice, there was
considerable variety, indicating a degree of vagueness in the original order. *(Crown Copyright/Air Historical Branch image CMP-846)*

▚ Armourers at RAF Luqa, Malta, prepare a bomb load for another raid on an Egyptian military target during Operation Musketeer. Canberra B.6, WH951, was the recipient of the weapons. By 30 October, five squadrons of Canberra B.6s and four squadrons of Valiant B.1s were present at RAF Luqa. *(Crown Copyright/Air Historical Branch image CMP-847)*

▚ Briefing crews at RAF Nicosia, Cyprus, on yet another raid on Egyptian military targets during Operation Musketeer. The board to the right indicates that crews from 18, 44, 115 and 10 Squadrons were involved with their Canberra B.2 aircraft. *(Crown Copyright/Air Historical Branch image NIC-RAF-4843G)*

Λ The scene at Nicosia during the early stages of the Suez action. Ten Canberra aircraft are seen taxiing out prior to a raid on military targets in Egypt. To the left are Valetta T.1 aircraft (probably of 114 Squadron) with Meteor NF.13 aircraft of 39 Squadron to the right. The special recognition stripes were, generally, applied to the aircraft while in Cyprus. When yellow paint ran out, ground crews applied cream emulsion, normally used to decorate the interior of quarters! *(Crown Copyright/Air Historical Branch image NIC-RAF-4849G)*

Other overseas activities

In 1956, in addition to the Suez Crisis, Britain was still involved in emergencies in Malaya, Kenya, Oman and Cyprus.

Thankfully, activities in Kenya were reaching their conclusion. In 1955 the Mau Mau terrorists were effectively defeated and the Avro Lincoln B.2 aircraft departed in July. At the end of September 1955, 1340 Flight was disbanded. During the Kenyan Emergency, RAF aircraft had dropped 21,936,201lbs of bombs and lost eight aircraft. On 17 November 1956, the army withdrew from Kenya, and in December the operational phase ended. By then, the war had cost the Mau Mau 10,527 dead and 2,633 captured; the security forces had lost 602 dead, of whom 534 were Africans. The British Government later calculated the cost of the emergency at precisely £55,585,424.

▲ At Blackbushe airfield on the morning of 12 January 1956 the first of twenty-eight Coastal Command Shackletons, drawn from eight squadrons, commenced the airlift of troops from the Parachute Regiment to Cyprus to counter the increasing threat of an uprising by Cypriot nationalists (EOKA). In addition to the usual lifejacket and other emergency equipment, each of the Shackletons' thirty-three passengers was also issued with ear plugs for the 14-hour flight to Nicosia via Malta. *(Crown Copyright/Air Historical Branch image PRB-1-11071)*

▼ Sabre F.4 fighters of 112 Squadron – including XB956/T and XB978/N, based at RAF Bruggen in Germany – carried the squadron's famous shark's mouth markings. 112 Squadron operated the Sabre F.4 from January 1954 to April 1956 as part of 2TAF and were photographed over Germany in January 1956. *(Crown Copyright/Air Historical Branch image CLP-225)*

Squadron Leader L.G. Bastard of 9 Squadron rolls off the top of a loop in his Canberra B.6, WH977, over the snow-covered Lincolnshire countryside during the display rehearsal on 18 January 1956. *(Crown Copyright/Air Historical Branch image PRB-1-11094)*

Squadron Leader L.G. Bastard of 9 Squadron pulls his Canberra B.6, WH977, round past the vertical of a loop prior to 'rolling off the top' during a rehearsal on 18 January 1956. The display was given at various locations during an upcoming tour of Africa by the squadron. *(Crown Copyright/Air Historical Branch image PRB-1-11086)*

Comet enters service

Despite the setbacks encountered by the original Comet 1 series, which entered service with BOAC on 2 May 1952, the type earned its place in history as the first turbojet aircraft in the world to operate regular commercial services. Similarly, the Comet Series 2, modified for service with the RAF, pioneered the use of the pure jet for military transport duties.

RAF Transport Command took delivery of fifteen Comets, beginning with XK670, which was delivered to RAF Lyneham on 7 July 1956. This aircraft, along with XK669, were originally designated Comet T.2s and employed for crew training. Subsequently, No 216 Squadron received eight Comet C.2s equipped as normal transport aircraft. Later, both T.2 variants were converted back to C.2 airframes.

216 Squadron's Comet aircraft had a significant impact on Transport Command's long-range abilities, making even the most distant parts of the Commonwealth within less than two days' travelling to the UK, and the Far East inside 24 hours.

De Havilland Comet C.2, XK669, in flight on 30 January 1956. The aircraft was still undergoing pre-service trials with de Havilland at the time of the photograph and was not delivered to 216 Squadron at RAF Lyneham until June 1956. *(Crown Copyright/Air Historical Branch image PRB-1-11159)*

Nine Hawker Hunter F.4 fighters (XE676/U, WV372/H, WV388/R, WV320/S, XE709/D, WV402/T, WV399/B, WV406/F and XE688/P) of 222 Squadron based at Leuchars, photographed in formation in February 1956. At the time, No 222 Squadron was in the process of swapping its original F.1 Hunters for the improved F.4 version. *(Crown Copyright/Air Historical Branch image PRB-1-11260)*

➤ This photograph serves to illustrate the three squadrons based at RAF Leuchars in February 1956. A Venom NF.3 (WX849) of 151 Squadron leads a formation of three aircraft. On the Venom's left wing is Hawker Hunter F.1, WW641, of 43 Squadron, while completing the trio is Hunter F.4 WV402/T from 222 Squadron (see photograph page 181). *(Crown Copyright/Air Historical Branch image PRB-1-11268)*

▼ Three de Havilland Venom NF.3s (WX849, WX864 and WX810) of 151 Squadron, RAF Leuchars, photographed in February 1956. The squadron's stint with the Venom was short-lived – having received its first aircraft in September 1955, the type was soon replaced by Javelin F(AW).5 aircraft in June 1957. *(Crown Copyright/Air Historical Branch image PRB-1-11271)*

The last operational jet squadron of the Royal Air Force to leave Egypt under the Anglo-Egyptian Suez Canal Zone Bases Agreement – No 208 (Fighter-Reconnaissance) Squadron with their Meteor FR.9s – making a farewell pass over the Pyramids. Commanded by Squadron Leader J.N. Thorne, the squadron had been based in Egypt intermittently since 1920, and the Sphinx forms the main part of the squadron badge. Special permission had been granted by the Egyptian Government for this flight. *(Crown Copyright/Air Historical Branch image CMP-806)*

Blackburn and General Aircraft Beverley C.1, XB263, pictured on 6 March 1956 when the aircraft was based at RAF Boscombe Down to undergo pre-service evaluation. *(Crown Copyright/Air Historical Branch image PRB-1-11321)*

⋀ Normally used for aircrew training, these Varsity T.1 aircraft (including WL675 in the foreground) had a 'date' with an atomic cloud in Australia. They formed part of a service task force comprising 500 men, Canberra jet bombers and helicopters taking part in nuclear tests at the Monte Bello Islands (Operation Grapple). One role allocated to the Varsity aircraft was the tracking of the cloud as it fell victim to the prevailing winds. The entire force gathered at Weston Zoyland in Somerset before reassembling in Australia on 27 March. The Canberra aircraft took air samples from the atomic cloud. The Force Commander was Group Captain S.W.B. Menaul, who was one of the RAF officers who had witnessed the US nuclear tests in Nevada in 1955. *(Crown Copyright/Air Historical Branch image PRB-1-11357)*

⋁ Eight Vickers Valiant B.1s (including WZ364 and WZ372) of 232 Operational Conversion Unit lined up at RAF Gaydon on 19 March 1956. 232 OCU formed at Gaydon on 21 February 1955 and was responsible for the training of all Valiant crews (and later, crews destined for the Victor) until it was disbanded on 30 June 1965. *(Crown Copyright/Air Historical Branch image PRB-1-11402)*

∧ Five Percival Jet Provost T.1s of 2 Flying Training School (2 FTS) at Hullavington peel away from the photographer during a sortie on 12 March 1956. These five aircraft (XD676/Q-U, XD678/Q-N, XD680/Q-T, XD692/Q-W and XD693/Q-Z) were part of the first batch of ten Jet Provost T.1s ordered by the RAF to prove the concept of a basic jet trainer. *(Crown Copyright/Air Historical Branch image PRB-1-11417)*

∨ From August 1955 trials were held at 2 Flying Training School at RAF Hullavington to prove the concept of an all-jet training programme. Side-by-side courses were run using both the Percival Provost T.1 (WV625/R-A pictured) and Jet Provost T.1 (XD693/Q-Z also pictured). The scheme proved successful and the first students to undertake all-jet training commenced flying at RAF Syerston in August 1959. *(Crown Copyright/Air Historical Branch image PRB-1-11426)*

▲ XD727/D, a Canadair-built Sabre F.4 of 92 Squadron, landing at RAF Linton-on-Ouse on 9 April 1956. *(Crown Copyright/Air Historical Branch image PRB-1-11555)*

▼ Supermarine Swift FR.5, XD907, photographed in flight along the south coast on 25 April 1956. XD907 never served with an operational squadron; instead it remained on the strength of the Handling Squadron at Boscombe Down for trials work between December 1955 and October 1959. *(Crown Copyright/Air Historical Branch image PRB-1-11562)*

Sunderland Vs of 201 Squadron based at Pembroke Dock, 3 May 1956. *(Crown Copyright/Air Historical Branch image PRB-1-11604)*

Sunderland Vs of 201 Squadron based at Pembroke Dock, photographed in flight on 3 May 1956. Having received the type in early 1945, they continued to fly the venerable aircraft until the squadron was disbanded at the end of February 1957. The aircraft nearest to the camera (SZ576/A-A) was sold to the French Navy in July 1957. *(Crown Copyright/Air Historical Branch image PRB-1-11601)*

⌐ An unusual formation of tactical reconnaissance aircraft
of the RAF and Royal Netherlands Air Force (RNAF) in
formation. This was photographed by a photo-
reconnaissance Meteor PR.10 of 541 Squadron during the
3rd NATO Central Region Reconnaissance Symposium,
held in May 1956. From the bottom: Supermarine Swift
FR.5, XD905 of 79 Squadron; English Electric Canberra
PR.7, WT758 of 31 Squadron; and Lockheed RT-33A
Shooting Star, TP-20, of the Royal Netherlands Air Force.
At the time of the photograph, 79 Squadron was based at
Wunstorf and was in the process of re-equipping with the
Swift FR.5, having flown the Meteor FR.9 since re-forming
at Gutersloh on 15 November 1951. *(Crown Copyright/Air
Historical Branch image CLP-238)*

➤ In April 1956, the 111 Squadron Hunter team had
been nominated as the official aerobatic team of No 11
Group and made their debut with a show at the French
National Air Display at Bordeaux on 12 May. Four Hunter F.4
aircraft, led by Squadron Leader Roger Topp in WV264/A,
are photographed in 'Box Four' formation while in a vertical
climb during a training flight on 4 May 1956. The remaining
team members were Flying Officer Dave Goodwin, Flight
Lieutenant George Aird and Flying Officer Dave Garrett.
(Crown Copyright/Air Historical Branch image PRB-1-11607)

Ʌ Personnel based at the Armament Practice Station at Sylt prepare a towed target for a gunnery practice sortie in May 1956. All of the Germany-based squadrons – including the Hawker Hunter F.4s of No 4 Squadron lined up in the rear of the photograph – made frequent visits to Sylt to hone their aerial firing skills. At the first Armament Practice Camp (APC) at Sylt in February 1956, attended by Hawker Hunter F.4s from Nos 98 and 118 Squadrons, 770 air gunnery sorties were flown in just fifteen days. Later APCs were attended by up to four squadrons at any one time; with up to 250 sorties flown per day. APCs normally lasted for one month; initial practice interceptions were flown against resident Vampire T.11s towing 25ft × 6ft banners, before moving on to the 25ft span glider (pictured above) towed by Meteors. *(Crown Copyright/Air Historical Branch image PRB-1-11807)*

ⱽ Lady Boyle, wife of the then Chief of the Air Staff, Sir Dermot Boyle, christens *Aries V*, a Canberra PR.7 (WT528) during a ceremony at the RAF Flying College at Manby on 14 June 1956. During its time with the college, WT528 set two world speed records. The first was Tokyo (Haneda airport) to London (West Malling) on 25 May 1957 (5,942 miles in 17 hours and 42 minutes, with an average speed of 335.7mph); the second was Washington DC (Friendship airport) to Caracas in Venezuela (Maiquiem airport) on 22 February 1958 (2,062 miles in 4 hours and 11 minutes, with an average speed of 491.95mph). WT528 was sold to the Indian Air Force in 1964. *(Crown Copyright/Air Historical Branch image PRB-1-11841)*

On 31 May 1956, eighteen Shackletons from Nos 42, 120, 204, 220 and 228 Squadrons formed the Queen's Birthday Flypast, flying over Buckingham Palace at 1,000ft in three separate formations. *(Crown Copyright/Air Historical Branch image PRB-1-11858)*

Farewell Lord Trenchard

On 10 February 1956, the RAF's first Chief of the Air Staff, Marshal of the RAF, Lord Trenchard GCB OM GCVO DSO, died aged 83. Today, Trenchard is recognised as one of the early advocates of strategic bombing.

Javelin enters service

The Javelin was the first twin-jet delta-wing fighter in the world and was designed to have a very high performance, with long endurance and the ability to intercept bombers flying at very high altitudes and high subsonic speeds. Electronic and radar devices enabled it to operate in all weather, day or night. The first prototype made its first flight at Moreton Valence on 26 November 1951. The first production Javelin F(AW).1 (XA544), made its maiden flight on 22 July 1954. A series of accidents with the six prototype aircraft delayed service entry, but the first of them were issued to 46 Squadron at RAF Odiham in February 1956. The F(AW).1 variant did not remain in service with 46 Squadron for long and was replaced in August 1957 by the improved F(AW).2, featuring American radar in a slightly shorter nose. Once again, these were short-lived and replaced in May 1958 by the improved F(AW).6 variant.

∨ The first Gloster Javelin F(AW).1s to enter service with the RAF joined 46 Squadron at Odiham in early 1956. The three aircraft pictured – XA620, XA627/B and XA628/Q – are from the first batch ordered by the RAF and were photographed in formation on 27 June 1956. A year later, 46 Squadron replaced the F(AW).1 with the improved Javelin F(AW).2 and transferred the 'old' aircraft to 87 Squadron in Germany. *(Crown Copyright/Air Historical Branch image PRB-1-11917)*

➤ Supermarine Swift FR.5, XD916, of 2 Squadron based at Geilenkirchen, Germany, photographed on 15 June 1956. This version of the Swift served with two squadrons of the 2nd Tactical Air Force in Germany – 79 Squadron being the other – from February 1956 until February 1961 when they were superseded by Hunter FR.10s. *(Crown Copyright/Air Historical Branch image CLP-241)*

◄ Four Canberra T.4 aircraft (WH843, XH584, WT485 and WH844) of 231 Operational Conversion Unit based at RAF Bassingbourn, rehearsing for a display at the Coventry Air Pageant held at Baginton Airport on 4 July 1956. Canberra WT485 was later sold to the Qatar Air Force in September 1975. *(Crown Copyright/Air Historical Branch image PRB-1-12025)*

➤ On 23 July 1956, HM the Queen carried out an official visit to RAF Marham where she presented a Standard to 207 Squadron. She later inspected examples of the Valiant, Vulcan, Victor and Canberra aircraft. The day concluded with a flypast of twenty Valiant and seventy-two Canberra aircraft. The lead section of the flypast is pictured here during a rehearsal for the event and consists of four Valiant aircraft based at Wittering and led by Wing Commander R.G.W. Oakley, Commanding Officer of 138 Squadron. After reforming at Gaydon in January 1955, No 138 Squadron was the first to receive Valiant B.1s when aircraft were delivered in the following month. 138 Squadron also took an active part in the Suez Campaign. *(Crown Copyright/Air Historical Branch image PRB-1-12071)*

The static display being prepared for a visit by HM the Queen to RAF Marham on 23 July 1956. Nearest the camera is a Victor B.1, XA921 and Vulcan B.1, XA889, along with eight Valiant B.1s, led by WZ389, in the line-up. Around twenty Canberra aircraft can also be seen towards the rear of the photograph. *(Crown Copyright/ Air Historical Branch image PRB-1-12226)*

Vulcan B.1 enters service

The prototype Vulcan (VX770) made its first flight on 30 August 1952. It represented the second of the new generation of long-range strategic V-Bombers to be ordered by the RAF. The first production aircraft (XA889) first flew on 4 February 1955. At the end of 1955, the Vulcan appeared with a modified plan-form, the chord at the wing-tips being increased, producing a compound taper to the leading edge which became known as the 'Phase 2 wing'.

The first Vulcan B.1 aircraft joined 240 Operational Conversion Unit (OCU) at RAF Waddington on 20 July 1956. The RAF's first operational squadron of Vulcan B.1s was with 83 Squadron in July 1957, once again at RAF Waddington.

Avro Vulcan B.1, XA891. This aircraft was the third production-standard Vulcan and was used primarily for engine installation tests by Bristol. It was also one of the first to be fitted with the distinctive kinked 'Phase 2' wing. The aircraft was destroyed in a crash near Walkington, Yorkshire, during a test flight on 24 July 1959. Thankfully all of the crew survived. *(Crown Copyright/ Air Historical Branch image PRB-1-12368)*

First 1,000mph aircraft

The Fairey Delta FD.2 supersonic research aircraft, WG774, set a world speed record of 1,132mph on 10 March 1956 – a record that was to remain until December 1957. The Fairey Delta 2 was also the first aircraft to exceed 1,000mph in level flight, an increase of around 300mph (480km/h) over the record set in August 1955 by a North American F-100 Super Sabre.

This record stood until 12 December 1957 when it was surpassed by a McDonnell JF-101A Voodoo of the United States Air Force.

In 1960, WG774 was rebuilt by British Aircraft Corporation (BAC) as the BAC 221 – for aerodynamic research as part of the Concorde development programme.

The Fairey Delta 2 supersonic research aircraft, WG774, which set a world speed record of 1,132 mph on 10 March 1956 – a standard that was to remain until December 1957. The Fairy Delta 2 was also the first aircraft to exceed 1,000mph in level flight. In 1960, WG774 was rebuilt by British Aircraft Corporation (BAC) as the BAC 221, for aerodynamic research as part of the Concorde development programme. WG774, in BAC 221 form, is now on display alongside the British Concorde prototype at the Fleet Air Arm Museum at Yeovilton. *(Crown Copyright/Air Historical Branch image PRB-1-12455)*

SBAC Show highlights

◄ English Electric Canberra B(I).8, XK951, pictured while participating in the 1956 SBAC Show at Farnborough. Shortly after the show, the aircraft joined 88 Squadron at Wildenrath in Germany. After serving with other German-based squadrons, the aircraft was later sold to Peru in April 1975 where it assumed the Peruvian Air Force identity '248'. *(Crown Copyright/Air Historical Branch image PRB-1-12459)*

➤ Single-seat Folland Gnat F.1, XK724, pictured while taking part in the 1956 SBAC Show at Farnborough. This aircraft was the first of six ordered by the Ministry of Supply for development flying, but the type was not purchased for the RAF. The aircraft's potential as a two-seat trainer was seen, however, and the Gnat became the standard fast-jet trainer with the RAF between 1962 and 1978, until it was superseded by the BAe Hawk T.1. The Gnat became famous as the first aircraft to be flown by the world-famous RAF Aerobatic Team, the Red Arrows and its predecessor the Yellowjacks, between 1965 and 1979. *(Crown Copyright/ Air Historical Branch image PRB-1-12461)*

◄ By the middle of 1956, the latest version of the RAF's Hawker Hunter single-seat fighter, the F.6, was ready to enter squadron service. Fitted with a more powerful Rolls-Royce Avon engine and improved flying controls, it was the most numerous version ordered for the RAF – some 379 being built and issued to fighter squadrons in Europe and the Middle East from October 1956. Its performance lent itself to aerobatics and many squadrons formed aerobatic display teams to showcase the Hunter's capabilities. Most notable of these was 111 Squadron which successfully looped twenty-two aircraft during the 1958 Farnborough display. This picture shows XG128, fitted with long-range tanks and carrying twenty-four rocket projectiles. XG128 was later modified as an FGA.9 variant. *(Crown Copyright/Air Historical Branch image PRB-1-12465)*

Farewell to the Lancaster

The last operational Avro Lancaster in RAF service, MR325/H-D, an MR.3 maritime reconnaissance aircraft operated by the School of Maritime Reconnaissance at RAF St Mawgan, was withdrawn from service following a short service on 15 October by the Station Commander, Group Captain D.R.S. Bevan-John. The aircraft was then flown to RAF Wroughton and placed in storage before being scrapped.

⋀ Farewell to the Lancaster. Group Captain D.R.S. Bevan-John, Station Commander at RAF St Mawgan, addresses a parade on 15 October 1956 to mark the retirement of the last Avro Lancaster in Royal Air Force service. The aircraft in question – RF325/H-D, a MR.3 maritime reconnaissance aircraft – was operated by the School of Maritime Reconnaissance and was flown to RAF Wroughton to be scrapped. The crew, led by Wing Commander E.J. Brooks, is lined up in front of the aircraft. *(Crown Copyright/Air Historical Branch image PRB-1-12539)*

⋁ Avro Lancaster MR.3, RF325/H-D – the last of the famous bombers to fly with the RAF – taxies out at St Mawgan on 15 October 1956 to the strains of 'Auld Lang Syne' for its final flight to RAF Wroughton to be scrapped. It was an ignominious end for such a long-serving aircraft. *(Crown Copyright/Air Historical Branch image PRB-1-12543)*

△ Lancaster MR.3, RF325/H-D, photographed on 15 October 1956 during its very last flight to RAF Wroughton. *(Crown Copyright/ Air Historical Branch image PRB-1-12545)*

First British Atomic Bomb dropped

On Thursday, 11 October, the first British nuclear weapon (named Blue Danube) was dropped from an RAF Valiant over Maralinga, South Australia, as part of Operation Buffalo. A small bomb, as such weapons go, it was equivalent in explosive power to 10,000 tons of TNT. The Valiant, from 49 Squadron, was led by Squadron Leader J.G. Flavell (captain), accompanied by Flight Lieutenants J.A. Ledger (co-pilot), E. Stacey (bomb-aimer), G.B. Spencer (navigator/plotter) and Flying Officer G.W. Ford (air electronics officer). The Valiant and its crew returned to RAF Wittering on 23 October.

▽ The crew of the 49 Squadron Valiant which carried out the first air drop of a British nuclear device on 11 October 1956. They did so during a series of tests at Maralinga, Australia, and they are pictured here on their return to Wittering on 23 October 1956. Left to right: Squadron Leader J.G. Flavell (captain), Flight Lieutenants J.A. Ledger (co-pilot), E. Stacey (bomb-aimer), G.B. Spencer (navigator/plotter), Flying Officer G.W. Ford (air electronics officer) and Chief Technician S. Lurcock (crew chief). *(Crown Copyright/Air Historical Branch image PRB-1-12650)*

Four Supermarine Swift FR.5 aircraft of 79 Squadron photographed while based at Gutersloh, Germany, on 14 November 1956. After reforming with Meteor FR.9s in November 1951, the squadron had recently re-equipped with the Swift. The Swift FR.5 was fitted with three oblique cameras for low-level tactical reconnaissance and a 220-gallon fuel tank in a bulged belly. It was also the first RAF aircraft to have a reheated engine. The ninety-four aircraft built served with Nos 2 and 79 Squadrons in Germany from February 1956 until March 1961. The Swift FR.5 was designed for pre- and post-strike reconnaissance of tactical nuclear targets and worked closely with Army Ground Liaison Officers (GLOs) attached to the squadrons. As no two-seat variants were available, pilots converted to type with sixteen 45-minute sorties alongside four days of ground school and three sorties in a flight simulator – one of the first flight simulators to be used by the RAF. Once on the squadron, pilots had to complete a further twenty-five representative operational sorties before being declared 'combat-ready'. A typical mission profile route included at least 250 miles at low level. High speed and low-level flying put a tremendous strain on the robust airframe, but the Swift was dogged in service by poor serviceability. *(Crown Copyright/Air Historical Branch image PRB-1-12710)*

➤ Six Hawker Hunter F.4s (including WV277/F, XE675/E, XE718/A, XE677/Q and WT760/C) of the 93 Squadron aerobatic team based at Jever, Germany, October 1956. Following the squadron's conversion from the Sabre F.4 in January 1956, the team was nominated to represent the 2nd Allied Tactical Air Force (2 ATAF) at displays on the Continent. *(Crown Copyright/Air Historical Branch image PRB-1-12727)*

⚠ Vickers Valiant B(PR)K.1, XD823, photographed in November 1956, shortly before joining 49 Squadron at Wittering. This version of the Valiant was one of a small number of aircraft converted to tankers which could also be fitted with cameras for strategic reconnaissance missions. It is painted in the white 'anti-flash' Titanite finish applied to the V-Force aircraft to offer some protection against the effects of a nuclear blast. *(Crown Copyright/Air Historical Branch image PRB-1-12812)*

⚠ Four Hawker Hunter F.6 fighters (XG233/J, XG232/G, XG226/D and XG229/F) of 92 Squadron, RAF Linton-on-Ouse, photographed on 30 November 1956. XG232 was later sold to the Chilean Air Force as 'J714' in July 1966. *(Crown Copyright/ Air Historical Branch image PRB-1-12824)*

➤ A superb air-to-air photograph of de Havilland Heron C.3, XH375, of the Queen's Flight, based at RAF Benson. *(Crown Copyright/Air Historical Branch image PRB-1-12876)*

A formation of three Gloster Javelin F(AW).1 fighters of 46 Squadron in flight from RAF Odiham in 1956. The aircraft are XA624/T, XA568/H and XA618/N. 46 Squadron equipped with the Javelin F(AW).1 in February 1956, but all were replaced by the F(AW).2 variant in August 1957. *(Crown Copyright/Air Historical Branch image T-273)*

▲ Another view of the three Gloster Javelin F(AW).1 fighters of 46 Squadron in flight from RAF Odiham in 1956. *(Crown Copyright/ Air Historical Branch image T-275)*

▼ A member of the groundcrew hands the pilot of 46 Squadron Gloster Javelin F(AW).1 XA571 his helmet, prior to departing RAF Odiham for a sortie in 1956. *(Crown Copyright/Air Historical Branch image T-283)*

A formation of three Gloster Javelin F(AW).1 all-weather fighters of 46 Squadron in flight from RAF Odiham, 1956. The three aircraft are XA624/T, XA568/H and XA618/N. *(Above: Crown Copyright/Air Historical Branch image T-307; left: Crown Copyright/Air Historical Branch image T-274)*

Beverley enters service

The Blackburn Beverley was introduced as a development version of the General Aircraft GAL 60 Universal Freighter which first flew in 1950. The first production Beverley (XB259) made its maiden flight at Brough on 29 January 1955 and forty-seven were built for the RAF before production ended in May 1958.

At the time of its introduction, the Beverley was not only the largest aircraft to enter RAF service but also the first British aircraft specifically designed for the dropping of heavy army equipment through rear-loading doors that could be removed for the purpose; as well as a variety of medium-range transport duties, offering high capacity and the ability to operate from small airfields. Unique features included a payload of almost 22 tons, a freight hold of nearly 6,000cu ft, a passenger-carrying tail boom and the remarkable take-off and landing runs of 810 yards and 350 yards respectively.

The Beverley C.1 first entered service with 47 Squadron at RAF Abingdon in March 1956 and served with the unit until retirement in October 1967.

Jeeps and trailers being loaded on to a 53 Squadron Blackburn Beverley C1, XB287/T at RAF Abingdon in the summer of 1956. At this time, equipment was being airlifted from the UK to join the Internal Security Flight based in Cyprus. *(Crown Copyright/ Air Historical Branch image T-295)*

A pair of 53 Squadron Blackburn Beverley C.1s, XB289/V and XB290/W, at RAF Abingdon in the summer of 1956. *(Crown Copyright/Air Historical Branch image T-298)*

1957

At the end of 1956, the backlash from Britain's intervention in Suez was disastrous. World opinion, especially that of the United States, together with the threat of Soviet intervention, forced Britain, France and Israel to withdraw their troops from Egypt. A United Nations peacekeeping force was sent in to supervise the ceasefire and to restore order. The Suez Canal was cleared and reopened, but Britain in particular found its standing with the US weakened and its influence east of Suez diminished by the adventure.

Accusations of collusion between Britain, France and Israel started in 1956, but were denied in parliament by Eden who tried to avoid giving a clear and categorical answer. He was at last asked whether there was foreknowledge of the Israeli attack and on 20 December, in his last address to the House of Commons, duly recorded in *Hansard*, he replied: 'I want to say this on the question of foreknowledge. And to say it quite bluntly to the House, that there was not foreknowledge that Israel would attack Egypt. There was not.'

In January 1957, his health shattered and his political credibility severely damaged, Sir Anthony Eden resigned. On 10 January 1957, he was replaced as British Prime Minister by Harold Macmillan.

Guy Mollet, the French Prime Minister, survived longer despite fierce criticism, but his government collapsed in June 1957 over taxation he imposed to pay for the Algerian War.

Anglo-American relations were strained by the Suez Crisis, but as Cold War Allies in NATO they continued to cooperate, and by 1963 Britain had adopted the US Polaris missile system. Nonetheless, the real balance of power in the post-war world had been starkly demonstrated and Britain's prestige had been dealt a severe blow.

⚠ The crew of a Vulcan B.1 bomber leave their aircraft as it is refuelled at RAF Waddington, Lincolnshire. The aircraft is XA896 of 230 Operational Conversion Unit. The first Vulcan aircraft to enter RAF service were allocated to 230 OCU for training and then 83 Squadron – both at Waddington – where this image was taken on 21 August 1957, shortly after the latter had reformed. XA896 is painted in the original silver scheme but was later painted overall white Titanite finish. To qualify as a captain on the Vulcan, pilots had to be assessed as 'above average', have flown at least 1,750 hours, have previous experience of four-engined aircraft and served on the Canberra. *(Crown Copyright/Air Historical Branch image T-337)*

'Reshape the forces, not mutilate them'

Under the new government of Harold Macmillan, Duncan Sandys was appointed Secretary of State for Defence on 14 January 1957. Speaking in a defence debate in the House of Commons on 13 February, Sandys said that his task was 'to reshape the forces, not to mutilate them.' He did not intend to 'slash about indiscriminately, lopping off bits and pieces here and there wherever it is easiest.' Any reductions made needed to be part of a coherent plan, and one which made sense both militarily and financially.

He went on to add that the superiority of the means of attack over those of defence, coupled with 'the catastrophic consequences of thermo-nuclear war' virtually determined the course that should be followed. 'The central theme of our policy must be to concentrate our military effort upon prevention rather than defence, to see that a thermo-nuclear war never happens,' he said.

Sanity in Bedlam

Following Sandys' speech, further unwelcomed and often uninformed speculation about the changing structure of Britain's defence forces continued until the then Chief of the Air Staff, Air Chief Marshal Sir Dermot Boyle, saw fit to offer his opinion in an attempt to counter much of the speculation.

Such was the feeling within the defence industry that the editor of *Flight* magazine – Maurice A. Smith – wrote a damning editorial on the subject in the 22 February 1957 edition, under the headline 'Sanity in Bedlam'. Part of it is reproduced here:

'Pity the poor public. The air-defence picture they are constrained to view, either out of good citizenship or sheer anxiety, is clouded enough by "security," doubt and indecision; but seen through a murk of "uninformed comment" and "authoritative views" it becomes utterly chaotic. Shadowy figures cry havoc or peace, mouth half-truths and blind assertions. The defence industry and the Armed Services appear puny, impotent, or superfluous as the fantastic light of politics and policies flickers around them. Faction rails against faction, "expert" against "expert", and only an uncommonly clear-sighted man can direct a light of truth on the confusion – a man like the Chief of the Air Staff, Air Chief Marshal Sir Dermot Boyle.

'Sir Dermot's declaration last week that loose talk about rockets making the Air Force obsolete was "terribly far from the truth" came as a ray of sanity upon a dark scene of bedlam. If there were a war in the next five years, he assured a Fleet Street audience, it would be fighters that would defend us. He implied that the change-over from aeroplanes to missiles would be a very gradual process and, most edifying of all, he gave it as his firm opinion that the RAF, with the help of scientists, would be able to defend our country – this in spite of a lot of people who insist that it is a waste of time to try to defend this land in the nuclear age.

'Any sensible person would be reluctant to predict a date for the final extinction of the manned fighter, but Sir Dermot's assurance of at least five years seems entirely reasonable. The English Electric P.1, upon which our air-defence system will be largely founded in the years ahead, could not possibly reach the squadrons for many months to come; and, notwithstanding the common assertion that the P.1 will be the RAF's last fighter, there is a certain rocket interceptor (doubtless the Saunders-Roe SR.53) which is known to be leading to another that "will probably be ordered in substantial quantities by the RAF".

'We echo the words of the Chief of the Air Staff: "At the moment the whole attitude of throwing away the things we know will work does not seem to be good sense".'

Duncan Sandys' Defence White Paper

On 4 April 1957, Duncan Sandys – the Secretary of State for Defence – stood up in parliament and presented his Defence White Paper which foreshadowed far-reaching changes in the RAF's strength and role. The shape of Britain's defence forces, the report pointed out, was largely settled by the rearmament launched in 1950 at the time of the Korean War. The ending of hostilities in Korea had radically altered the position. The immediate danger of war had receded, but had been replaced by the prospect of a long period of acute international tension. It had also become apparent that a military effort on the scale planned in 1950, envisaging expenditure of £4,700 million over three years, was way beyond the country's capacity.

The White Paper went on to discuss specific aspects of vital concern to the RAF. It must be frankly recognised, it pointed out, that there was at the time

∨ Avro Vulcan B.1, XA895, pictured at Boscombe Down while undergoing trials with the Handling Squadron in January 1957. XA895 was later converted to a B.1A variant. *(Crown Copyright/Air Historical Branch image PRB-1-13011)*

∧ A line of 284 Squadron Bristol Sycamore HC.14s waits to depart Nicosia, Cyprus, for a troop-drop in the Kyrenia Mountains during an exercise with the King's Own Yorkshire Light Infantry. It was held for the benefit of the national press on 16 January 1957 to highlight the methods of troop insertion during the ongoing EOKA nationalist campaign. 284 Squadron-equipped Sycamore helicopters pioneered the techniques of night flying and landing troops by abseiling down ropes from a hovering helicopter. In addition, the squadron dropped food, ammunition and stores, as well as evacuating 222 casualties from the hills and forest areas of Cyprus during the conflict with the EOKA. *(Crown Copyright/Air Historical Branch image CMP-873)*

no means of providing adequate protection for the people of the UK against the consequences of nuclear attack. In the event of war, though the British fighters should be able to take a heavy toll of enemy bombers, a proportion would inevitably get through. Even if it were only a dozen, they could, with nuclear weapons, inflict widespread devastation. This made it even clearer than ever that the overriding consideration in all military planning was to prevent it, rather than prepare for it.

The White Paper also stated that a fighter force smaller than that then in existence would be maintained and progressively equipped with air-to-air guided missiles. Then came an ominous statement: 'Fighter aircraft will in due course be replaced by a ground-to-air guided missile system.' More than fifty years on, further fighter development has shown this statement was somewhat premature!

The report went on to detail the reduction in the 2nd Tactical Air Force in Germany to around 50 per cent of its size by the following March. To offset the reductions, some of the squadrons remaining would be provided with nuclear weapons. A similar reduction in size would be made to the light bomber force based in England that was assigned to NATO.

Later, the Minister of Labour, Mr Iain Macleod, said in the House of Commons that he estimated there would be a reduction of 'some 15,000' workers in the aircraft industry during the next twelve months as a result of the planned defence cuts. That was to prove something of an understatement! Although later ministers reversed the policy, the lost orders and cuts in research were responsible for several British aircraft manufacturers going out of business. That impact of the Sandys White Paper was to prove irreversible. A very large section of Britain's once-great aviation industry would be gone forever.

Overseas activities

In 1957, Britain was involved in emergencies in Malaya, Oman and Cyprus. Britain has long maintained close links with Oman through a succession of treaties to protect her oil interests and sea routes. In 1952, a small force of Vampire FB.5s, along with a Valetta transport aircraft, had been deployed to Sharjah to police the disputed border with Saudi Arabia. After demonstrations and leaflet-drops, talks began and the aircraft returned to Iraq in October. In 1953, after talks had stalled, the

➤ Although there are no clues in the official records of 245 Squadron as to why this signed photograph from Hawker of the prototype Hunter, WB188, should have been presented to them, it is, however, a unique piece of aviation memorabilia. The squadron received its first Hunter F.4s around this time of the presentation as replacements for the last Meteor F.8s serving with Fighter Command, only for the unit to be disbanded on 1 June 1957! The names on the photograph are a veritable 'Who's Who' of British test pilots with the signatures of Duncan Simpson, David Lockspeiser, Frank Bullen, Hugh Merewether and Bill Bedford all present. *(Crown Copyright/Air Historical Branch image AHB-MIS-H613)*

aircraft retuned to Sharjah to prepare a blockade on the Saudi infringement. The Vampires were soon replaced by four Meteor FR.9s as the Vampire FB.5s had suffered in the dusty environment; although the Meteors did not fare any better in the conditions. Two Lancaster GR3s were deployed from Malta but these could hardly be spared from NATO commitments in the Mediterranean. In the following years, a variety of RAF aircraft were involved in the conflict, including Valettas, Lincoln B.2s, Ansons, Pembroke and Venom FB.1 aircraft.

In 1957, the Omani Liberation Army (OLA) terrorist activities increased, particularly around Jebel Kaur. Venom FB.4s of Nos 6 and 249 Squadrons were moved to Sharjah while Beverleys and a Valetta from 84 Squadron, along with two Shackletons of 37 Squadron, were detached to Sharjah from Bahrain. From 24 July the Venoms began attacking forts at six locations, including Nizwa, Tanuf and Firq. Forty-eight hours earlier, Shackletons had dropped warning leaflets. The peak of air activity was on 30 July when Meteor FR.9s of 208 Squadron and a Canberra PR.7 also participated. After a period of softening up from the air, ground forces moved into the area on 7 August to occupy the forts. The OLA now withdrew to the impenetrable Jebel Akhdar, a fertile plateau at over 7,000ft with few easily guarded approaches. From here the OLA presented less of a threat, and most British forces withdrew; although this was not to be the end of the conflict in Oman as trouble was to flare up again in February 1958.

Royal Auxiliary Air Force disbanded

Despite the major restructuring and reorganisation of the force back in 1954, it was announced on 10 March 1957 that all Royal Auxiliary Air Force squadrons would be disbanded, effectively reducing RAF Fighter Command's strength by twenty squadrons.

Buckets of sunshine – Operation Grapple

On 15 May 1957, the first British hydrogen (thermonuclear) bomb (code named Short Granite) was dropped by a Valiant from No 49 Squadron and exploded off Malden Island in the Pacific. The Valiant BK.1 used for the test – XD818 – was captained by Wing Commander K.G. Hubbard, OC 49 Squadron.

The base at Christmas Island had been prepared by the army the previous year with the construction of twenty-five miles of roads, and by RAF and army airfield

Britain's first thermonuclear bomb (Short Granite), which was exploded off Malden Island on 15 July 1957. *(Crown Copyright/Air Historical Branch image AHB-MIS-XMAS-13)*

construction engineers of a 7,000ft runway for bombers and an auxiliary landing strip. Thousands of tons of heavy equipment were taken by sea, while mail and fresh food were flown in from Honolulu by RAF Hastings transport aircraft.

A number of brand-new Valiant BK.1 aircraft were specially modified for the Operation Grapple task – XD818, 822, 823, 824 and 825. The additional equipment included extra protection to the crew (and the on-board scientific instrumentation) against the heat and radiation. Most of the aircraft were delivered to 49 Squadron

⋀ The four Valiant aircraft (BK.1s XD818, 822, 823 and 824) and crews of 49 Squadron, which deployed to Christmas Island in the Pacific to conduct the first series of British thermonuclear bomb tests (Operation Grapple), gathered at Wittering on 1 March 1957 prior to their departure. The aircraft received several modifications for the tests, including reinforcements to the airframe to withstand the blast, and blinds in the cockpit to protect the pilot and co-pilot from the glare. *(Crown Copyright/Air Historical Branch image PRB-1-13081)*

in November 1956. In addition to the Valiant aircraft, Shackleton, Dakota and Canberra aircraft were involved in the operation and based at Christmas Island ahead of the test. The Shackleton aircraft provided maritime reconnaissance capabilities to ensure the test area was clear, while the Canberra aircraft carried special 'sniffing' equipment to sample the bomb's mushroom cloud. The Dakota aircraft provided valuable transport capabilities.

The weapon was dropped from precisely 45,000ft, with an airspeed of Mach 0.76 on a heading of 203° true. In order to achieve the correct drop, precision flying from the crew was absolutely essential. After the weapon was released, the crew flew the required escape manoeuvre.

At around 2½ minutes after the bomb was dropped, the crew of XD818 experienced the shock waves, although relatively mild in nature. Five minutes later the crew were allowed to remove anti-flash screens in order to observe the development of the fireball and mushroom cloud effect.

The Valiant B.1 used in the first test – XD818 – is now preserved with the Royal Air Force Museum collection at RAF Cosford.

A A small detachment of RAF Transport Command Hastings aircraft were maintained at Christmas Island. These regularly made the journey to and from Honolulu carrying mail and fresh vegetables. *(Crown Copyright/Air Historical Branch image AHB-MIS-XMAS-F36)*

➤ An aerial view of the base at Christmas Island which had been prepared by the army the previous year. Visible in this image are four Valiants, eight Canberras, two Dakotas and a single Shackleton aircraft. *(Crown Copyright/ Air Historical Branch image AHB-MIS-XMAS-12)*

➢ A graphic representation of the escape manoeuvre required to get Valiant BK.1 XD818 away from the explosion as quickly and safely as possible during the Operation Grapple test off Malden Island on 15 July 1957, when Short Granite was dropped. *(Crown Copyright/Air Historical Branch image AHB-MIS-XMAS-10)*

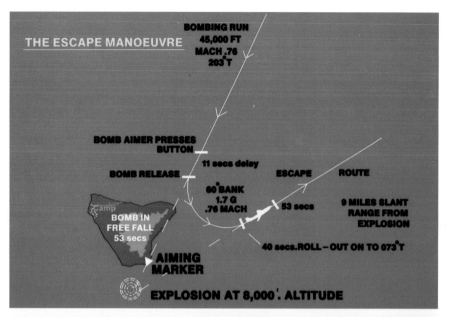

➢ Another graphic representation of the bombing circuit used for the Operation Grapple test on 15 July 1957. The northern marker was made of bulldozed coral, as was the southern marker. The target indicator was made of a bulldozed coral arrow pointing towards a Day-Glo red triangle painted onto a black background. *(Crown Copyright/Air Historical Branch image AHB-MIS-XMAS-15)*

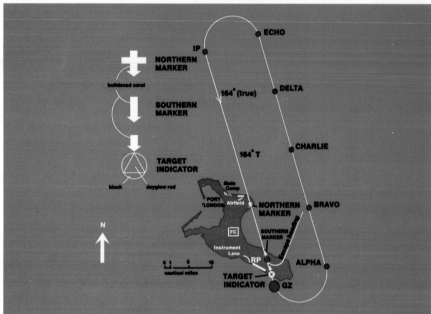

➢ Another graphic representation of the location of the various assets employed during the Operation Grapple test on 15 July 1957. *(Crown Copyright/Air Historical Branch image AHB-MIS-XMAS-27)*

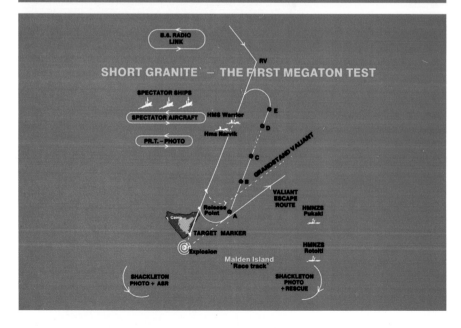

The tented accommodation of the main camp at Christmas Island. *(Crown Copyright/Air Historical Branch image AHB-MIS-XMAS-26)*

Farewell to the Avro York

RAF Changi, Singapore, said goodbye to the last of the RAF's venerable four-engined Avro York C.1 aircraft – MW295, named *Ascalon II* – which flew around 300,000 miles in the Far East during the three years it had been based in Singapore. It left Changi for RAF Aldergrove, Northern Ireland, in April 1957. *Ascalon II* had been flown to Singapore in April 1954 by Squadron Leader Douglas Boards, who flew the aircraft throughout its stay at Changi. Squadron Leader Boards, who was the personal pilot to the Commander-in-Chief Far East Air Force, Air Marshal Sir Francis Fressanges, described the aircraft as 'wonderfully reliable'.

⋀ RAF Changi, Singapore, said goodbye to the last of the RAF's venerable four-engined Avro York C.1 aircraft – *Ascalon II* – in 1957. Squadron Leader Douglas Boards, who flew it throughout its stay at Changi, described the aircraft as 'wonderfully reliable'. MW295 was operated by the Far East Communications Squadron. *(Crown Copyright/Air Historical Branch image CFP-958)*

ᐱ Members of the crew of a Vickers Valiant B.1 aircraft talk with local children at an airfield in Ghana (possibly Takoradi) in March 1957. The crew was one of four from 207 Squadron which flew from their base at RAF Marham to participate in the Ghanaian independence celebrations and give a series of aerial demonstrations over Accra and regional capitals. *(Crown Copyright/ Air Historical Branch image T-3)*

ᐯ Four Hunter F.4s of 43 Squadron – WV324/U, WV366/T, WV387/Q and XF299/O – displayed as the 13 Group Hunter Aerobatic Team in 1956. Shortly after this picture was taken in 1957, the team represented the RAF at an air show in Rome on 24 June to mark the opening of Fiumicino airport, the finale of which featured two pairs of Hunter aircraft landing simultaneously at opposite ends of the runway and passing one another at the half-way point directly in front of the grandstand. The outward flight to Rome was not without incident, however, as two aircraft suffered cracked windscreens due to bird-strikes and a third had a rudder which 'fell off at Istres', requiring a visit from a team of engineers from Fighter Command to mend it before the journey could continue. The team also had the distinction of performing in front of a Russian delegation at RAF Marham, which included the Russian Premier Marshal Bulganin, his deputy Nikita Khrushchev and the famous aircraft designer A.N. Tupolev. *(Crown Copyright/ Air Historical Branch image T-9)*

▲ The sole military registered example of the Percival Jet Provost T.2, XD694, in a 1957 publicity shot. This aircraft was the last of ten development aircraft ordered in 1953 to validate the concept of a jet-powered basic training aircraft modified to eradicate some of the issues found in the earlier Jet Provost Mark 1. It was fitted with shorter undercarriage legs, as the original units were occasionally prone to 'wobble' when taxiing. A more powerful Viper engine was fitted in a redesigned rear fuselage. The aircraft spent its time at 2 Flying Training School (2 FTS) at Hullavington with the early T.1 aircraft and was eventually withdrawn from service at the end of 1959. *(Crown Copyright/Air Historical Branch image PRB-1-13146)*

➤ Helicopters played a crucial role in the campaign in Malaya, where they were used initially to recover wounded troops from small jungle clearings and latterly for troop placement. Westland Whirlwind HAR.4 of 155 Squadron is seen here on troop-lifting operations with men of the RAF Regiment (Malaya) in the state of Selangor on 18 April 1957. *(Crown Copyright/Air Historical Branch image CFP-967)*

◄ De Havilland Devon C.1, VP958, of the Metropolitan Communications Squadron based at RAF Hendon flying over Greenwich with the Docklands area of London below, March 1957. *(Crown Copyright/Air Historical Branch image PRB-1-13173)*

▽ Examples of the two types employed by Fighter Command in the late 1950s, photographed in formation in April 1957. Nearest the camera is a Gloster Javelin F(AW).4, XA636, of 141 Squadron based at RAF Horsham St Faith (now Norwich airport) with Hawker Hunter F.6, XF440/D, of Odiham-based 247 Squadron leading. At the time, 141 Squadron was in the process of completing its conversion from the Venom NF.3 and was declared operational on its new mount in the following month. *(Crown Copyright/Air Historical Branch image PRB-1-13328)*

An unidentified Hawker Hunter F.4 of 74 Squadron being rearmed at RAF Horsham St Faith, Norfolk, on 25 May 1957. The detachable gun pack on the Hawker Hunter enabled the turnaround time between sorties to be reduced to as little as seven minutes. *(Crown Copyright/Air Historical Branch image T-207)*

Armourers fitting a Fireflash air-to-air beam-riding radar-guided missile to the wing pylon of Supermarine Swift F.7, XF122, at the Guided Weapons Development Squadron at RAF Valley, 18 June 1957. The Fireflash was the UK's first air-to-air guided missile and had two solid-fuel rocket motors capable of propelling the missile in excess of Mach 2. It was only issued in very limited numbers by the RAF. *(Crown Copyright/Air Historical Branch image PRB-1-13459)*

▲ Four Piston Provost T.1s of the Central Flying School aerobatic team The Sparrows, in tight formation on 2 July 1957. The aircraft in this view are XF837/P-C, XF607/X-G, XF892/P-B and XF609/X-K. The team were formed to represent the CFS at the SBAC Show at Farnborough in September 1957. *(Crown Copyright/Air Historical Branch image PRB-1-13516)*

▼ Pilots and navigators of 141 Squadron walk past their Javelin F(AW).4 all-weather fighters on returning to RAF Horsham St Faith, Norfolk, after a sortie on 24 June 1957. In the foreground is Javelin F(AW).4 XA639, followed by XA750 and XA761. *(Crown Copyright/Air Historical Branch image PRB-1-13699)*

⋀ Groundcrew of 141 Squadron prepare one of the squadron's Gloster Javelin F(AW).4 aircraft, XA759, for a night sortie from RAF Coltishall in 1957. *(Crown Copyright/Air Historical Branch image T-244)*

⋁ Smoke from the engine-starting cartridges of Gloster Javelin F(AW).4, XA754, of 23 Squadron, engulfs the aircraft and groundcrew as the aircraft prepares for a sortie from RAF Coltishall. 23 Squadron moved to Coltishall on 28 May 1957 and operated the Javelin F(AW).4 until July 1959. *(Crown Copyright/Air Historical Branch image T-250)*

Groundcrew work on 148 Squadron Vickers Valiant BK.1, XD819, at RAF Marham. The BK.1 variant of the Valiant had started to arrive with 148 Squadron at Marham in December 1956 and remained on squadron strength until December 1964.
(Crown Copyright/Air Historical Branch image T-252)

RAF engineers servicing the number 3 engine of a Blackburn Beverley transport aircraft at RAF Abingdon in mid-1957.
(Crown Copyright/Air Historical Branch image T-285)

➤ Westland Whirlwind HAR.2, XJ766, is unloaded from Beverley C.1 XB289/V of 53 Squadron at Abingdon, Oxfordshire, in June 1957 when the helicopter returned to the UK having served with the Internal Security Flight and 284 Squadron in Cyprus. *(Crown Copyright/Air Historical Branch image T-293)*

A Handley Page Hastings C.1 (TG614) of 70 Squadron runs up its engines prior to take-off from an airfield in the Middle East – probably Nicosia – in July 1957. *(Crown Copyright/Air Historical Branch image CMP-903)*

▲ A pair of Blackburn Beverley C.1s (including XB283/G) of 47 Squadron, Transport Command, at Khormaksar, Aden, in July **1957.** *(Crown Copyright/Air Historical Branch image CMP-905)*

▼ A Gloster Meteor FR.9 – VZ602/T – fighter reconnaissance aircraft of 208 Squadron at Sharjah in the Trucial States (now the United Arab Emirates). 208 Squadron were detached here in July and August 1957 during the troubles in Oman.
(Crown Copyright/Air Historical Branch image CMP-908)

⋀ An Avro Shackleton MR.2, WL737/D, of 42 Squadron at Sharjah. Shackletons carrying fragmentation bombs were in action in Oman during RAF operations against the OLA rebels. WL737 was later converted to an AEW.2 variant. *(Crown Copyright/Air Historical Branch image CMP-909)*

⋁ Avro Shackleton MR.2, WR951/E, of 42 Squadron, pictured at Sharjah during operations against Yemeni rebels on the Yemen–Aden border in 1957. *(Crown Copyright/Air Historical Branch image CMP-912)*

▲ A de Havilland Venom FB.4 fighter, WR518/F, of 8 Squadron at Sharjah, during a series of operations against dissident Yemeni tribesmen on the Aden–Yemen border, 1957. *(Crown Copyright/Air Historical Branch image CMP-915)*

▼ A Bristol Sycamore HR.14 helicopter of 284 Squadron lands at a remote location near the deserted village of Livadhi, Cyprus, during a routine patrol. *(Crown Copyright/Air Historical Branch image CMP-920)*

▲ Avro Vulcan B.1, XA896, photographed while being refuelled at RAF Waddington after returning from a training sortie on 21 August 1957. XA896 was the fourth Vulcan to join 230 Operational Conversion Unit, having been delivered to the unit on 7 March 1957. *(Crown Copyright/Air Historical Branch image T-340)*

▼ An early colour image of Blackburn Beverley C.1 XB284/H in flight. At the time of its introduction in March 1956, the Beverley was not only the largest aircraft to enter RAF service, but also the first designed for the dropping of heavy army equipment through rear-loading doors which could be removed for this purpose – as seen in this view. *(Crown Copyright/Air Historical Branch image T-429)*

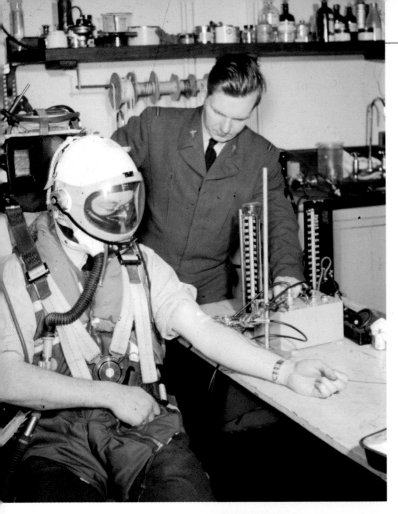

◄ A member of staff at the Institute of Aviation Medicine at RAF Farnborough is seen wearing a helmet and other flying clothing during a test of pressure breathing equipment in the High Altitude (Respiratory Research) Section, mid-November 1957. A medical officer checks the readings during the test. *(Crown Copyright/Air Historical Branch image T-456)*

➤ An officer of the Institute of Aviation Medicine at RAF Farnborough photographed in the gondola of the institute's centrifuge undergoing 'g' tests in November 1957. He is only wearing a partial g-suit with chest and lower body equipment and helmet. *(Crown Copyright/Air Historical Branch image T-457)*

Highlights of the SBAC Show

The SBAC Show held at Farnborough from 2–9 September was another large display of British aviation ability. The highlight of the show was the appearance of the English Electric P.1B prototype XA847 which had only made its first flight in April. Two Gloster Javelin F(AW).7 aircraft (XH710 and 714) also appeared at the event. This was the RAF's latest version of the aircraft powered by a pair of more powerful Sapphire 7 engines, each of 11,000lbs thrust, and was the first variant of the type to be equipped with Firestreak missiles as standard. The 1957 SBAC event also featured a much larger air display with numerous service flypasts from the Royal Navy and RAF, as well as a spectacular formation display from the 111 Squadron Hunter F.6 display team, the Black Arrows, which included a perfect nine-ship formation loop and roll before separating for the normal five-ship display.

The second prototype Avro Vulcan, VX777, taking off from Farnborough during the annual SBAC Air Show, September 1957. *(Crown Copyright/Air Historical Branch image PRB-1-13879)*

Major-General William H. Blanchard, Commander of the 7th Air Division, United States Air Force, accompanied by the Air Officer Commanding-in-Chief Bomber Command, visited RAF Waddington on 23 September 1957. They were there to meet the crews of Valiant and Vulcan jet bombers who would be taking part in the forthcoming USAF Strategic Air Command's Bombing, Navigation and Reconnaissance Competition at Pinecastle AFB, Florida, between 30 October and 5 November 1957. In the foreground is an RAF Vulcan with General Blanchard's B-47E 52-0334 to the rear. *(Crown Copyright/Air Historical Branch image PRB-1-13892)*

⋀ The first Vulcan B.1 aircraft to enter RAF service were allocated to 230 Operational Conversion Unit for training and then 83 Squadron – both based at Waddington – where this image was taken in September 1957, shortly after the latter had reformed. The two furthest aircraft, XA900 and XA901, are painted in the original silver scheme worn by the first Vulcan B.1 aircraft, while those closer to the camera (XA905, 906 and 907) are painted in the overall white Titanite finish. *(Crown Copyright/Air Historical Branch image PRB-1-13950)*

◄ Three Waddington-based Vulcan B.1s in line-astern formation, during a photoshoot in September 1957. *(Crown Copyright/Air Historical Branch image PRB-1-13959)*

An impressive mix of aircraft types in use with the Empire Test Pilots' School at Farnborough on 25 April 1957. On display are a Devon (XA879/2), a Royal Navy Gannet, three Meteors (including T.7s WA638/8 and WL488/11 and an NF.11, WD797), a Hunter F.1 (WT621), Vampire trainer and Piston Provost (WV425). At this time, the school had fifteen different aircraft types on its books. *(Crown Copyright/Air Historical Branch image PRB-1-14153)*

Shackleton MR.2s of 228 Squadron lined up at Luqa, Malta, in June 1957. The crews were undergoing anti-submarine training when detached to the island for Exercise Fair Isle. *(Crown Copyright/Air Historical Branch image CMP-937)*

Handley Page Hastings C.1, TG551/GAN, wearing the colours of 99 Squadron based at RAF Lyneham, photographed in flight in September 1957. 99 Squadron had equipped with the Hasting C.1 and C.2 back in August 1949 and continued to operate the type until June 1959 when they were replaced by the Bristol Britannia C.1 and C.2. The large 'GAN' letters on the side of the fuselage are the aircraft's VHF radio call-sign. *(Crown Copyright/Air Historical Branch image T-474)*

De Havilland Comet C.2 XK697 from 216 Squadron at RAF Lyneham, photographed in September 1957. It was during this month that the squadron commenced regular flights to Christmas Island in the Pacific where a base had been built to carry out the first drop of a British-built thermonuclear weapon. The route took in stops at Keflavik (Iceland), Goose Bay (Canada), Offutt Air Force Base (Nebraska), Travis AFB (California), Honolulu (Hawaii) and Christmas Island. *(Crown Copyright/Air Historical Branch image T-513)*

A 216 Squadron crew are put through a training sortie in a Comet flight simulator at Lyneham, Wiltshire, in September 1957. *(Crown Copyright/Air Historical Branch image T-501)*

De Havilland Comet C.2 XK697 from 216 Squadron at RAF Lyneham photographed in September 1957. *(Crown Copyright/Air Historical Branch image T-515)*

First flight of the P.1B

On 4 April 1957 the English Electric P.1B prototype (named Lightning in October 1958), XA847, made its first flight. The single-seat fighter had twin Rolls-Royce Avon 200 series turbojets with reheat, providing a thrust of over 20,000lbs, which allowed the aircraft to exceed the speed of sound in level flight. It was reported that it regularly exceeded the former world air speed record of 1,132mph in the course of routine test flights. It could be armed both with 30mm Aden guns and de Havilland Firestreak guided missiles, and quantity production of the P.1B was ordered as the future equipment of Fighter Command. Around the time, it was stated that 'it will be the last manned fighter of the RAF but that its useful life will extend for seven to ten years'. The first deliveries to 74 Squadron were made in June 1960, and 11 Squadron had the F.6 until April 1988 – slightly longer than some politicians had anticipated!

▽ The English Electric P.1B Lightning prototype, XA847, made its first flight on 4 April 1957. The single-seat fighter had twin Rolls-Royce Avon turbojets with reheat and exceeded the speed of sound in level flight. *(Crown Copyright/Air Historical Branch image PRB-1-14369)*

Creation of the Memorial Flight at Biggin Hill

On 11 July 1957, the RAF's last three Spitfire PR.19 aircraft from the former THUM Flight at RAF Woodvale – PM631, PS853 and PS915 – were flown from Duxford to Biggin Hill to mark the creation of the Memorial Flight, which would later become the RAF Battle of Britain Memorial Flight. To mark the occasion, a presentation speech was made by the Air Officer Commanding-in-Chief Fighter Command, AM Sir Thomas Pike. At Biggin Hill the last three airworthy Spitfires joined the RAF's last airworthy Hawker Hurricane, LF363.

The Victor enters service

The first Handley Page Victor B.1 to enter RAF service joined No 232 OCU at RAF Gaydon on 29 November 1957. The Victor was the last of three types of aircraft ordered for the re-equipment of the RAF under the British V-Bomber programme. The first operational unit, No 10 Squadron at RAF Cottesmore, received the first of their aircraft in April 1958.

1958

Sputnik, Thor and Bloodhound

For many, 1958 was the year of the Sputnik. For the RAF, however, it was the year in which American Thor offensive intercontinental ballistic missiles were added to Bomber Command's armoury and British Bloodhound defensive ground-to-air guided missiles to that of Fighter Command. The first event shook the confidence of the Western World in their supposed superiority over Russia in the field of rocket development; the last two shook the faith of some RAF flying men in the supposed superiority of manned aircraft over missiles.

On 1 July 1958, the first Bristol-Ferranti Bloodhound Mk.1 radar-homing surface-to-air missile for area defence entered service with No 264 Squadron at RAF North Coates. Originally developed under the code name Red Duster, it was propelled by two Bristol-Siddeley Thor ramjets at a speed of Mach 2 after being launched by four Gosling rocket-boost motors. It was deployed in units of sixteen in Air Defence Missile Squadrons of Fighter Command in defence of V-Bomber or Thor bases.

➤ **Two Avro Vulcan B.1 bombers pictured at the Royal Australian Air Force station at Butterworth, Malaya, during a detachment by 83 Squadron from Waddington, Lincolnshire, in November 1958.** *(Crown Copyright/Air Historical Branch image T-764)*

The Air Staff had not intended for Bloodhound to take the place of manned fighters, but to operate in conjunction with them. Similarly, in spite of the formation of the first Intermediate Range Ballistic Missile (IRBM) squadron – No 77 at RAF Feltwell in Bomber Command on 19 September – they did not expect the missiles to replace the Valiant bombers that were operating at most of the squadrons, while the Vulcan and Victor bombers with their improved performance, were also entering service in increasing numbers.

A White Paper issued on 13 February 1958 revealed that the USA would supply Thor IRBMs for Bomber Command, together with the specialised equipment required to operate the system, and training assistance. The agreement was to remain in force for five years unless it was terminated by either government giving six months' notice.

'They can fly as high and as fast as any bomber in service in any country', the 1958 Defence White Paper stated, 'and their navigation and bomb-aiming equipment is of the highest accuracy'. In addition, good progress was being made with the development of self-propelled weapons – the so-called 'stand-off' bomb – which could be released at a considerable distance from the target, thereby making it unnecessary for the manned aircraft to fly into the more heavily protected target area.

As for Thor, the 'Wingless Deterrent', as it had been called, had emerged from being shadowy paper projects to becoming a series of 'thunderous metal cylinders' by the middle of 1958. Produced by the Douglas Aircraft Company of America, its length was 62ft, it had a range of 1,500 miles, and in the course of its flight would reach a maximum speed of around twelve times the speed of sound. Its two most obvious shortcomings, compared with the V-bombers, were its vulnerability to attack on the ground (as it could not be dispersed from its permanent base in times of international tension) and its lack of flexibility (as it could not be transferred to an overseas theatre of operations).

A Thor squadron consisted of fifteen missiles and 600 officers and men. The fifteen launch pads were normally located in five groups of three with each trio being effectively a self-contained unit. One complex of power generators, fuel tanks and power distribution trailers handled one group of three missiles while the launch-control trailer, with its associated radar, processed three countdown stations – one per missile.

Around this time, there were great arguments in military and aviation circles concerning the British Government's military missile policy. A *Flight* magazine editorial from 1958 suggested that, 'Britain more than any other country, seems to have fallen into the trap of regarding military aircraft and missiles as direct competitors, fighting each other for the money available.'

'We say again', commented another *Flight* editorial, 'that the famous, or infamous, White Paper by the British Ministry of Defence in April of last year merely provided an essential jolt; it should not, and could not, have signified any sudden lack of interest in manned aircraft. Britain will have to have manned military aeroplanes for years to come: and somebody had better start ordering them.'

Another feature published in *Flight* magazine told the story of the Avro Vulcan. 'The perceptive foresight and remarkable courage of the British Air Staff' who, shortly after the end of the Second World War, had formulated a requirement for a bomber having twice the speed and operating altitude of the Lincoln, the then current RAF long-range bomber. The specification that A.V. Roe and Co. drew up turned out in the end to be the most successful of the V-bombers; and the Vulcan was appreciably in advance of aircraft in the same role across the world. In May 1958, a further order was placed for the English Electric P.1B which was announced in the House of Commons by the then Minister of Supply, Mr Aubrey Jones. So, thankfully, the immediate future outlook for manned aircraft in the RAF was less gloomy than the depression caused by the 1957 White Paper had led many people to think.

▲ The first Victor B.1 to arrive in Bomber Command was XA931, which was delivered to Gaydon on 28 November 1957 for 232 Operational Conversion Unit. The aircraft was photographed after landing back at its Warwickshire base in April 1958. 232 OCU was responsible for the training of both Valiant and Victor crews while 230 OCU at RAF Waddington trained Vulcan aircrew. Three of the early Victors (XA923, 924 and 925) were fitted with special equipment and were soon transferred to the Radar Reconnaissance Flight at Wyton to replace Valiant aircraft used on 'special duties', of which little is known. April 1958 also saw the formation of the first Victor squadron – 10 Squadron at RAF Cottesmore – which received its first aircraft on 9 April. *(Crown Copyright/Air Historical Branch image PRB-1-14592)*

▼ Vickers Valiant B.1, XD869, of 214 Squadron based at RAF Marham, Norfolk, taxiing at a snow-covered Gaydon, Warwickshire, on 13 January 1958. XD869 only served with 214 Squadron and crashed during a night take-off from Marham on 11 September 1959. *(Crown Copyright/Air Historical Branch image T-527)*

⋀ RAF V-Force bombers. An Avro Vulcan B.1A, XA904, leads a Vickers Valiant BK.1 (XD869) and a Handley Page Victor B.1 (XA931) in flight on 13 January 1958. The Vulcan is in the combined colours of 83 Squadron and 230 Operational Conversion Unit, both based at Waddington, Lincolnshire. XD869 is from 214 Squadron based at Marham, Norfolk, and XA931 is from 232 Operational Conversion Unit of Gaydon, Warwickshire. The white 'anti-flash' colours are typical of the early days of V-Bomber operations. *(Crown Copyright/Air Historical Branch image T-528)*

⋁ The same three RAF V-Force bombers at altitude on 13 January 1958. *(Crown Copyright/Air Historical Branch image T-531)*

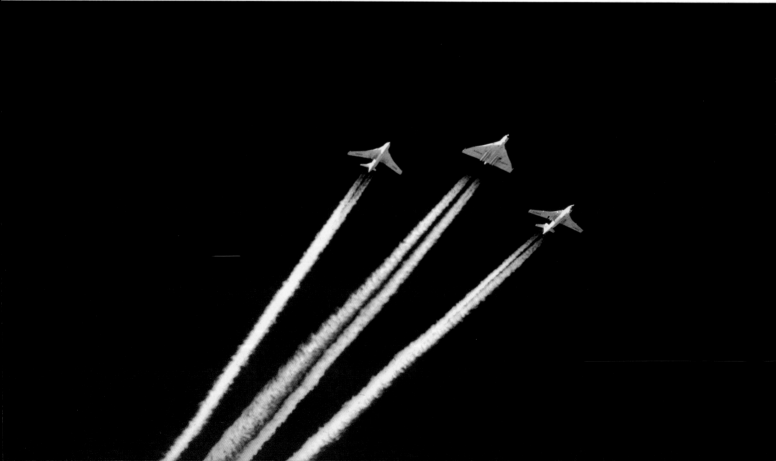

⋀ The crew of Handley Page Victor B.1, XA931, of 232 Operational Conversion Unit, leave their aircraft after landing back at their home station at Gaydon, Warwickshire, on 13 January 1958. *(Crown Copyright/Air Historical Branch image T-545)*

⋁ Handley Page Victor B.1, XA931, of 232 Operational Conversion Unit, deploys its brake parachute after landing back at its home station at Gaydon, Warwickshire, on 13 January 1958. XA931 was the fifteenth production Victor B.1 and the first to enter service with the RAF, being received by 232 OCU at Gaydon on 28 November 1957. It joined 'A' Squadron, which had the responsibility of converting RAF crews onto the new bomber. XA931 later served with 10 Squadron before returning to 232 OCU and being struck off charge on 30 April 1974. *(Crown Copyright/Air Historical Branch image T-546)*

Λ During the late 1950s, the concept of air-to-air refuelling was developed by the RAF as a means of extending the range of both its bombers and fighters. The Vickers Valiant became the RAF's standard tanker aircraft until the mid-1960s. Two Valiant B(PR)K.1s – WZ376 and WZ390 – were used for trials by Vickers-Armstrong and were photographed during a test flight on 12 February 1958. Note the cutaway bomb bay and rear fuselage of the refuelling aircraft (WZ376) to accommodate the hose drum unit (HDU or 'Hoodoo') and the air-to-air refuelling hose and drogue. *(Crown Copyright/Air Historical Branch image PRB-1-14667)*

➢ XA853 was the second of three prototypes of the English Electric P.1B, seen here carrying two de Havilland Firestreak infrared homing missiles during a flight in May 1958. These are mounted on launching 'shoes' on short pylons either side of the forward fuselage. *(Crown Copyright/Air Historical Branch image PRB-1-15081)*

A practice scramble by a crew of 10 Squadron with a Handley Page Victor B.1 at RAF Cottesmore in April 1958. *(Crown Copyright/Air Historical Branch image T-1018)*

A mass of black smoke and spray from a wet flightline at RAF Stradishall is kicked up following a simultaneous start by Javelins of various squadrons at the Suffolk station on 13 January 1958. The aircraft are drawn from Nos 89, 41 and 23 Squadrons, based at RAF Stradishall and Coltishall respectively. The nearest aircraft, XA815, was the first of thirty-three Javelin F(AW).6s delivered to the RAF fitted with an improved AI22 air interception radar. *(Crown Copyright/Air Historical Branch image PRB-1-15171)*

Hunting Jet Provost T.3 aircraft of the CFS Jet Aerobatic Team based at RAF Little Rissington during a photoshoot on 28 May 1958. The aircraft were painted in this special red and white colour scheme at RAF St Athan to emphasise the difference between the top and bottom surfaces in anticipation of being able to do part of the routine flying inverted. *(Crown Copyright/Air Historical Branch image T-575)*

Another view of the four Hunting Jet Provost T.3 aircraft of the CFS Jet Aerobatic Team during a photoshoot on 28 May 1958. The team flew seventeen displays during the 1958 season, including the SBAC Show at Farnborough in September. *(Crown Copyright/Air Historical Branch image T-576a)*

Overseas activities

In 1958, Britain was still involved in emergencies in Malaya, Oman and Cyprus.

Towards the end of 1957, the OLA took the initiative in Oman and almost captured Tanuf. The Sultan's Armed Forces (SAF), with RAF help, attempted to oppose them, but this failed. Instead, a blockade was attempted to stem the flow of arms to the otherwise impenetrable Jebel Akhdar, although the British Government was not keen to get drawn into a major confrontation. In February 1958, two 17,000-yard 5.5-inch Howitzer guns were set up and began shelling the summit villages, while the RAF concentrated on attacking the water supply in the hope of disrupting the pattern of life so that the villagers would deny support to the OLA. The attempt appeared to be failing, leading the RAF to step up its bombing campaign. In one week in September, Shackleton aircraft dropped 148 1,000lb bombs, while Sea Hawks and Sea Venoms from HMS *Bulwark* joined the action for a few days. Finally, 22 SAS Regiment were brought in from Malaya in preparation for an assault on the plateau in early 1959.

Photographic survey of Aden

Following many months of flying by RAF Valiant, Canberra and Meteor aircraft, the 112,000-square mile photographic survey of Aden Colony and Protectorate, carried out for the Colonial Office and Directorate of Military Survey, was successfully completed in January 1958.

First flight of the Wessex

Following the cancellation of the tandem-rotor Type 191 by the Admiralty, Westland turned to the Sikorsky S-58 for a solution to the Royal Navy's requirements, earlier having successfully worked with the licensed production of the Sikorsky S-51 and S-55 helicopters. Westland received a USN HSS-1N Seabat anti-submarine helicopter, powered by a Wright radial engine. This was assembled and test-flown to obtain standard performance figures. The 1,525hp Wright radial engine was removed and a 1,100shp Napier Gazelle NG.11 free-turbine turboshaft engine installed, which provided an improvement in performance over the Wright-powered version, as well as being half its weight.

Development work continued under a Ministry of Defence contract and three pre-production aircraft were ordered (XL727–729). A further eight pre-production aircraft (XM299–301 and XM327–331) were then ordered. One of these was used to incorporate another development, with a pair of coupled 1,350shp Bristol-Siddeley Gnome engines installed in the nose of the helicopter in place of the single Napier Gazelle shaft-turbine. This made its first flight on 20 June 1958 with Westland's Chief Test Pilot 'Slim' Sear at the controls. This version would become the HC.2 variant for the RAF and orders were placed in August 1961 for transport, ambulance and general-purpose duties, including ground assault with Nord anti-tank missiles and machine guns. The Wessex would play a significant role in the RAF over the coming years.

◄ Scottish Aviation Pioneer CC.1, XJ466, of 267 Squadron pictured on 13 May 1958. At the time of the photograph, 267 Squadron was based at Kuala Lumpur as the communications squadron for the Air Headquarters Malaya. They flew a variety of light transport and communications aircraft including the Pioneer, Harvard, Dakota, Auster and Pembroke throughout the region in support of the ongoing Operation Firedog. *(Crown Copyright/Air Historical Branch image CFP-979)*

Help for Jordan

From 1955, the Soviet Union provided military aid to both Egypt and Syria, including the supply of aircraft and the building of airfields in Syria. These airfields, located in the west of Syria, clearly threatened Lebanese and Jordanian integrity. In February 1958, the United Arab Republic (UAR) was formed between Egypt and Syria. Simultaneously, Iraq and Jordan agreed to an anti-communist, anti-Nasser Federation. The situation at the eastern end of the Mediterranean grew more tense with revolt in Lebanon, and following the assassination of the Iraqi Prime Minister Nuri al-Said on 15 July, King Hussein of Jordan appealed to Britain the following day for assistance in maintaining stability.

The request was immediately supported and on the following morning 200 troops were moved to Amman from Cyprus by Hastings aircraft of 70 Squadron. For a time they seemed to be isolated, since Israel temporarily refused permission for further overflights. After pressure from the US Government, Israel relented and successive flights of RAF transport aircraft were escorted by US Navy fighters from the Sixth Fleet.

By 18 July, 2,200 troops were in Amman with light artillery support. Reinforcements had been flown into Cyprus by Comet C.2s of 216 Squadron, assisted by Shackleton aircraft drawn from 42 and 204 Squadrons. Beverley C.1 aircraft flew in heavy equipment from Cyprus. The troops were followed by a detachment of Hunter F.6 aircraft from 208 Squadron on 20 July from Akrotiri.

King Hussein established a pledge of loyalty from the powerful Bedouin tribes on 11 August and British troops began withdrawing after a UN resolution called for an end to Western intervention later in the month. The last British troops left on 2 November 1958.

Beverley C.1 transport aircraft at Nicosia, Cyprus, during the airlift of British forces into Jordan in July 1958. *(Crown Copyright/ Air Historical Branch image CFP-965)*

A A Beverley C.1 (foreground) and Hastings aircraft (including C.1 TG612 and C.2 WD487) at Nicosia, Cyprus, during the airlift of British forces to Jordan in July 1958. *(Crown Copyright/Air Historical Branch image CFP-971)*

SBAC Show highlights

With the continuing contraction of the British aircraft industry, the number of new designs and total aircraft participating in the event was noticeably down. Significant service participation by the RAF and Royal Navy, however, helped to make this a great event. Highlights included the first appearance of the two prototype Blackburn NA.39 aircraft (XK486 and 487); the prototype Canberra U-10 remote-controlled target drone (WJ624) converted from the B.2 (later designated D.10, of which eighteen were converted); and the second prototype of the de Havilland Sea Vixen F(AW).1 (XJ475).

The flying display was quite spectacular! No fewer than forty-five Hawker Hunters flew in formation, as did a similar number of Gloster Javelin aircraft. The three new V-bombers – Valiant B.1 XD862, Vulcan B.1 XA911 and Victor B.1 XA935 – passed over in formation, while two more Valiant aircraft – XD812 (Tanker) and WZ930

(Receiver) – both from 214 Squadron, demonstrated the type's new air-to-air refuelling capabilities.

Without doubt, the highlight of the show was the never-to-be-repeated spectacle of a formation loop by twenty-two Hawker Hunter aircraft from 111 Squadron, led by Squadron Leader Roger Topp. The incredible feat was achieved by using additional aircraft and pilots from other squadrons. One astonished journalist recorded: 'a mass of aircraft heading low towards the airfield, which suddenly reared up to reveal no less than 22 Hunters performing a perfectly aligned loop'. The formation then completed a second loop, with six aircraft being shed and the remaining sixteen rolling in formation. A further seven were then shed, and the remaining nine were looped, with four more breaking away to complete a bomb-burst loop and leaving five aircraft to finish the show.

➤ Sixteen Hunter F.6s of 111 Squadron photographed while rehearsing in August 1958 for the forthcoming SBAC Show at Farnborough. The famous display team was led by Squadron Leader Roger Topp and, after 'borrowing' aircraft and pilots from other squadrons, the team actually looped twenty-two aircraft in formation at Farnborough, a never-to-be-repeated spectacle. *(Crown Copyright/Air Historical Branch image PRB-1-15606)*

➤ Having looped and rolled sixteen Hunter F.6 fighters in formation at the 1957 SBAC Show at Farnborough, 111 Squadron decided to go six better for the following year's event and repeat the feat with twenty-two aircraft. The squadron is seen rehearsing for the air show and the additional aircraft (borrowed from other front-line squadrons) required to achieve this spectacular formation are easily recognizable as they had not been painted into the famous all-black colours used by 'Treble One' at this time. *(Crown Copyright/Air Historical Branch image PRB-1-15707)*

⋀ The second pre-production English Electric Lightning F.1, XG308, in flight around the time of the 1958 SBAC Show at Farnborough. *(Crown Copyright/Air Historical Branch image PRB-1-15639)*

⋁ To improve the forward view for the pilot during landing, the Fairey Delta 2 supersonic research aircraft had the ability to lower its long nose. This was demonstrated by the pilot during a photographic sortie around the time of the 1958 SBAC Show at Farnborough (see also page 194). *(Crown Copyright/Air Historical Branch image PRB-1-15643)*

⋀ The Hawker Hunter F.6 was the standard day fighter in service with the RAF and one of the type – XE618 – was photographed during its appearance at the 1958 SBAC Show at Farnborough. *(Crown Copyright/Air Historical Branch image PRB-1-15657)*

⋁ The RAF's advanced jet trainer throughout the 1960s and 1970s was the Folland Gnat T.1. The aircraft was originally designed as a single-seat low-cost fighter and two of that variant, the Gnat F.1, were photographed while participating in the 1958 SBAC Show at Farnborough. The aircraft nearest the camera is XK741 and is fitted with a full complement of external stores; two 66-gallon drop-tanks and twelve 3in rocket projectiles. A 30mm Aden gun was also fitted on the lip of the starboard engine air intake. The additional fuel tanks were specially designed for the Gnat and had a curved profile to improve aerodynamic airflow over the rear control surfaces. The second aircraft in the photograph was flying as G-39-10. XK741 is now displayed at the Midland Air Museum at Coventry as GN-101. G-39-10 was later sold to the Finnish Air Force where it operated as GN-103, and is now on display in the Aviation Museum of South-Eastern Finland. *(Crown Copyright/Air Historical Branch image PRB-1-15662)*

The first operational squadron to form on the Victor B.1 was No 10 at Cottesmore in April 1958. Eight of the squadron's aircraft (including XA940, XA938, XA935, XA929 and XA937) are pictured at their home station on 10 September 1958. A number of aircraft including XA937 and XA938 were later converted into air-to-air tankers as the BK.1 variant and later, the K.1. *(Crown Copyright/Air Historical Branch image PRB-1-15698)*

A Westland Dragonfly helicopter of the Central Flying School Helicopter Squadron landing at South Cerney on 26 August 1958. The Westland Dragonfly was the first British-built helicopter used by the **RAF.** *(Crown Copyright/Air Historical Branch image PRB-1-15736)*

➤ A pair of Gloster Javelin F(AW).5 aircraft from the Central Fighter Establishment at RAF West Raynham provided flying displays at the Kenya Agricultural Show, which took place from 1–4 October 1958, and then made a liaison visit to the Royal Rhodesian Air Force from 6–8 October that year. *(Crown Copyright/Air Historical Branch image PRB-1-15743)*

∨ An airman removes the protective covers from the first Thor IRBM handed over to the RAF at RAF Feltwell, Norfolk, on 19 September 1958. *(Crown Copyright/Air Historical Branch image PRB-1-15750)*

⋀ Supermarine Swift F.7, XF124, of the Guided Weapons Development Squadron (GWDS) based at RAF Valley, Anglesey, carrying Fairey Fireflash air-to-air missiles during a test flight on 2 October 1958. Only twelve F.7s were built, ten of which were used by GWDS for air-to-air missile development between April 1957 and December 1958, when they were withdrawn.
(Crown Copyright/Air Historical Branch image PRB-1-15795)

⋁ The crew of a Valiant bomber 'scramble' during a visit to RAF Wyton by HRH the Duke of Edinburgh, 24 June 1958.
(Crown Copyright/Air Historical Branch image T-654a)

➤ Student navigators of 2 Air Navigation School, based at RAF Thorney Island, under instruction in a Vickers Valetta T.3 in September 1958. *(Crown Copyright/Air Historical Branch image T-671)*

⩔ A flight of three English Electric Canberra B6s (WH948, WT210 and WH958) of 12 Squadron, based at RAF Binbrook, Lincolnshire, photographed in the air in September 1958. Note what appears to be a replacement leading edge to the starboard wing of WH948 where the serial has not been completely repainted. *(Crown Copyright/Air Historical Branch image T-716)*

Aircraft and personnel of 208 Squadron detached from Akrotiri, Cyprus, to Amman, Transjordan, in October 1958. The aircraft, three Hawker Hunter F.6s, are XE599/C, XF441/P and XF436/H. *(Crown Copyright/Air Historical Branch image T-723)*

A Handley Page Hastings C.1 of 36 Squadron (but still wearing the markings of 511 Squadron) taxies into position at Amman, Transjordan, in October 1958. *(Crown Copyright/Air Historical Branch image T-725)*

⋀ The Royal Air Force in Jordan in 1958. Hawker Hunter F.6s of 208 Squadron, Middle East Air Force, were based at Amman, Jordan, from July to November 1958. *(Crown Copyright/Air Historical Branch image CMP-1013)*

⋁ Following a UN resolution calling for the end of Western intervention in August 1958, British Forces were withdrawn from Jordan. A Jordanian officer watches a Transport Command Beverley C.1 (probably from 84 Squadron) taxiing in at Amman to collect another load of troops and equipment. On the left are Hunters of 208 Squadron, and in the background is a Hastings of 70 Squadron. The last British troops left on 2 November 1958. Flight magazine, in their 14 November 1958 edition, recorded that during the five-day airlift more than 2,000 troops and RAF personnel were moved. The eight Beverley and Hastings aircraft flew ninety round trips between Amman and Cyprus, covering 58,000 miles in 310 hours. The force used a 10 mile-wide corridor over Lebanon and Syria under UN supervision. One Beverley was intercepted by Syrian Air Force MiGs without further incident.
(Crown Copyright/Air Historical Branch image CMP-1014)

Firestreak operational

Originally known by the code name Blue Jay, the Firestreak air-to-air infra-red homing missile was developed by the de Havilland Propeller Company from 1951. In October 1958, the Firestreak was introduced into RAF service, fitted to the latest Gloster Javelin F(AW).7 aircraft of RAF Fighter Command. The missile was guided by an infra-red seeker cell behind its glass nose, which locked onto the target before launch from the parent aircraft. The 50lb high-explosive warhead was detonated by a proximity fuse.

St Clement Danes

On 19 October 1958, St Clement Danes in the Strand was reconsecrated as the church of the Royal Air Force by the Archbishop of Canterbury, in the presence of Her Majesty Queen Elizabeth II and HRH the Duke of Edinburgh. On 10 May 1941, the church had been severely damaged and reduced to charred remains by Luftwaffe incendiary bombs. The church was originally built by Sir Christopher Wren in 1682, on the foundations of far older churches, the first of which had been built by Danes who were married to English women at the time of Alfred the Great.

Following an appeal for funds by the Royal Air Force, Commonwealth and Allied Air Forces, the church was completely restored. More than 700 squadron and unit badges made of Welsh slate were let into the floor, together with a memorial to Polish squadrons. Beneath the north gallery is a memorial to the 19,000 members of the United States Air Force who gave their lives while flying from British soil. In the simple chapel in the crypt, the black granite font came from the Royal Norwegian Air Force, the paschal candelabrum from the Royal Belgian Air Force and the stone altar was the gift of the Royal Netherlands Air Force. The RAF Church of St Clement Danes is a fitting memorial to the men and women of many countries who fought and flew with the RAF during the Second World War.

Ⓥ Avro Vulcan B.1, XH497, of 617 Squadron, photographed in the air on 10 October 1958. Interestingly, XH497 had its nose wheel fall off on take-off on 5 July 1958. The aircraft landed on its main wheels and the nose wheel leg. The aircraft was repaired and served until 1966 when it was withdrawn. *(Crown Copyright/Air Historical Branch image PRB-1-15981)*

⋀ Scottish Aviation Pioneer CC.1, XK368, of 267 Squadron, pictured while delivering supplies to the jungle outpost at Fort Shean, Malaya, in November 1958. The Pioneer's short take-off and landing capabilities made it an ideal type for use in the Far East where rough airstrips in jungle clearings were used for resupply missions to the numerous remote locations throughout the country. *(Crown Copyright/Air Historical Branch image PRB-1-16210)*

⋁ Blackburn Beverley C.1, XB265/A, of 47/53 Squadron, pictured at Abingdon, Oxfordshire, with a Scottish Aviation Pioneer CC.1, XL557, of 215 Squadron. *(Crown Copyright/Air Historical Branch image T-257)*

Avro Shackleton MR.2 WR960/X of 228 Squadron, RAF Coastal Command, in flight near its base at St Eval, Cornwall. 228 Squadron reformed at St Eval on 1 July 1954 and took delivery of its first Shackleton MR.2s in the same month. The squadron moved to RAF St Mawgan on 29 November 1956, before returning to St Eval in January 1958. The Shackleton MR.2 remained with the squadron until it was disbanded in March 1959. *(Crown Copyright/Air Historical Branch image T-326)*

Towards the end of 1958, six Westland Whirlwind HAR.2 helicopters were sent from the UK to Cyprus. This was carried out to provide additional helicopters for 284 Squadron during a period of increased security following a resumption of the insurgency by EOKA nationalists. The Whirlwinds, from the Joint Experimental Helicopter Unit based at Middle Wallop, were flown out on Beverley aircraft (C.1 XB268 here) of Transport Command to perform internal security patrols over the island. One of the helicopters, XK968, is pictured being unloaded after arriving at Nicosia. *(Crown Copyright/Air Historical Branch image CMP-1040)*

➤ British forces based in Cyprus were reinforced at the end of 1958 to counter the increased activity of EOKA nationalists. Having reformed at RAF Hullavington on 20 November 1958, 114 Squadron and its Chipmunk T.10 aircraft were almost immediately transported to the island to undertake security patrols while based at Nicosia, remaining there for four months before disbanding at the end of the conflict on 14 March 1959. *(Crown Copyright/ Air Historical Branch image CMP-1042)*

Chipmunk T.10, WK586, of 114 Squadron, patrolling the coastline of Cyprus at Kyrenia in December 1958. *(Crown Copyright/Air Historical Branch image CMP-1048)*

Twin Pioneer enters service

The outstanding success of the single-engined Pioneer in service with the RAF at home and overseas led to the decision in 1956 to order the larger twin-engined aircraft from the same manufacturer – Scottish Aviation. The Twin Pioneer first appeared as a sixteen-seat passenger aircraft, which made its first flight on 25 June 1955. The initial order for the RAF was for twenty Twin Pioneer CC.1 aircraft, similar to the civil Series 1, and the first military version flew on 29 August 1957. The contract was increased to thirty-two aircraft and, later still, to thirty-nine – the last seven aircraft being designated Twin Pioneer CC.2. This version was similar to the CC.1 and differed only in some minor structural changes. The last three aircraft were military equivalents of the civil Series 3 with more powerful Alvis Leonides engines of 640hp. Later, in 1961, all Twin Pioneers were retrofitted to this standard.

Twin Pioneers, or 'Twin Pins' as they were often referred to, were first supplied to No 78 Squadron in Aden in October 1958, where they served alongside the Pioneer CC.1. The Twin Pioneer inherited all the STOL characteristics of its single-engine predecessor, needing an area of only 300 yards by 100ft to operate. The Twin Pioneer remained in service with 78 Squadron until June 1965, although the type officially remained in RAF service until the end of 1968.

TSR-2 announced

The year 1958 ended on a high. On 17 December, the Secretary of State for Air announced, 'It has been decided to develop a new strike/reconnaissance aircraft as a replacement for the Canberra. This will be capable of operating from small airfields with rudimentary surfaces and have a very high performance at all levels.' This aircraft was later designated the TSR-2. Sadly, the project would later be cancelled before the potentially world-beating aircraft could even enter service with the RAF.

How times have changed

An interesting snippet appeared in the 21 March 1958 edition of *Flight* magazine. It is reproduced below in its entirety:

'Fewer aircraft for M.o.S.?'
    'Following questions by Sir Frank Tribe, the Comptroller and Auditor-General, on the number of aircraft used by the Ministry of Supply for research and development flying and other duties, the total of these machines was reduced last year from 637 to 604 – including 138 on loan, 420 allotted to research and development, and 18 for communications. The value of the 604 aircraft (as assessed in October 1957) was £50m. Annual running costs, including fuel, spares and maintenance, were £5m.
    'Sir Frank says (in his report, published recently, on the appropriation accounts) that the Ministry had told him it might be possible to manage with fewer aircraft.'

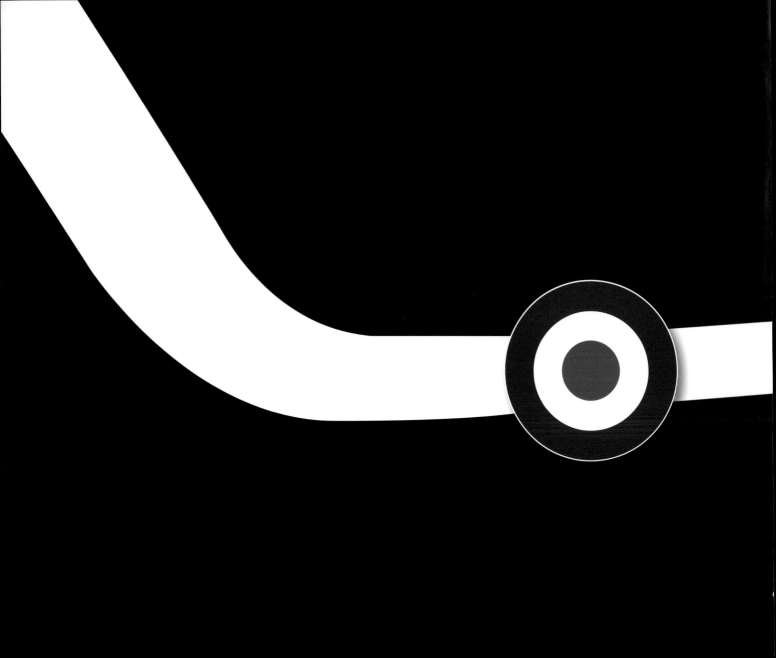

1959

Oman conflict reaches a conclusion

In 1959, the RAF was still involved in emergencies in Malaya, Oman and Cyprus. With the arrival of D Squadron of 22 SAS Regiment into Oman from Malaya, activities against the OLA were on the increase. As the unit settled down to probing the approaches and determining its tactics, it was joined by A Squadron and a number of Kenyan trackers. The final assault was made on the night of 26/27 January 1959 and the plateau was reached before dawn after a magnificent climb during which ropes were used. By 30 January, the key villages of Saiq, Habib and Sharayah were occupied.

From 9 February, the SAS and RAF units were withdrawn but 152 Squadron, which had formed from 1417 Flight in the previous October, remained at Muharraq to support the SAF.

➤ Bristol Britannia C.1, XL636 *Argo*, of 99 Squadron, photographed during a flight from Lyneham, Wiltshire, in 1959. The Royal Air Force ordered a total of twenty-three Britannia aircraft and the first (XL635) made its first flight on 29 December 1958. *(Crown Copyright/Air Historical Branch image T-1078)*

Cyprus

The problems with the EOKA in Cyprus, under the leadership of the ex-Greek colonel George Grivas, continued into 1959. All three services – Army, Fleet Air Arm and Air Force – were involved during the year. The British Army had a number of Auster AOP.6 aircraft with 653 Squadron operating from Nicosia on general reconnaissance and liaison work. A number of airstrips had been prepared across the island until fifteen were in regular use by the hard-working unit. The Fleet Air Arm provided Gannet AS.1 and AS.4 aircraft from 847 Naval Air Squadron, based at Nicosia, to monitor shipping in the area in order to prevent arms smuggling to EOKA.

In 1959, the RAF's 284 Squadron were operating out of Nicosia. From October 1956, 284 Squadron had been involved in the conflict in Cyprus, operating their Sycamore HR.14 helicopters, primarily in support of army ground forces. These were later supplemented by Whirlwind HAR.2 helicopters from the Joint Experimental Helicopter Unit (JEHU).

Towards the end of 1958, British military strength had increased and there were diplomatic moves to end the conflict. The spiritual leader of the Greek Community –

Archbishop Makarios – suspected of supporting EOKA, had been deported in 1956, but he was released in Athens in April 1957. He announced his abandonment of support for Enosis in September 1958. Following a London conference in February 1959, Archbishop Makarios was allowed to return to Cyprus.

Cyprus was a conflict in which the helicopter came into its own. Despite their limited payload, the Sycamores were able to place troops quickly in inaccessible parts of the mountainous countryside, thereby keeping EOKA units constantly on the move. By the time the emergency ended in December 1959, 284 Squadron had been operating continuously in support of the army since 1955. In all, 284 Squadron flew 9,729 hours in 19,375 sorties, dropping 4,000 troops and 120 tons of supplies. They also lifted 268 casualties.

In 1958, when Field Marshal Lord Hastings handed over the Governorship of Cyprus to Sir Arthur Foot, he said that 284 Squadron had 'contributed more to fighting terrorism on the island than any other single unit'.

➤ **The first Hunting Percival Jet Provost T.3, XM346, pictured while flying with the Aeroplane and Armament Experimental Establishment (A&AEE) at Boscombe Down, 5 April 1959. This was the first version of the Jet Provost to be widely issued to training units having received several modifications, including shortening of the undercarriage legs, which were prone to 'wobbling' when taxiing at high speed.** *(Crown Copyright/ Air Historical Branch image PRB-1-16475)*

Live firing of Thor missile

The Thor was a stop-gap nuclear deterrent available from the United States which operated on a 'dual-key' basis. In early January 1959, the first launch crew of 98 Squadron assembled at the Douglas Aircraft Company at Tucson, Arizona, for a training course. Little did they realise that they would make history by being the first RAF crew to launch a Thor missile.

After completion of the training course, the RAF crew moved to Vandenburg Air Force Base in California where the first RAF Thor missile was delivered to them. After checking and rechecking of all the systems and components, a launch date of 14 April 1959 was set. A number of technical issues, along with less-than-ideal weather, prevented an on-time launch. The shelter was finally moved back to reveal the missile in its white gloss finish and RAF roundel before it was raised into its vertical launch position.

At approximately 09.00 hours on 16 April, the launch sequence recommenced. Further delays were experienced, due to a minor technical issue along with low cloud, and the countdown continued. Except for a slight delay in liquid oxygen loading, the countdown continued almost perfectly. An amber light lit up indicating that the engines were about to start and within five seconds they had developed the full 150,000lbs of thrust, which lifted the 65ft missile from its launch pad. Smoke and flames at the emplacement almost obliterated the television view, but immediately reports started to pour in from visual observers that lift-off was normal and that the missile was climbing within programmed limits. The RAF had launched its first surface-to-surface ballistic missile.

◄ A Thor IRBM seen here raised on its launch pad at a Bomber Command station in March 1959. In early January 1959, the first launch crew of 98 Squadron assembled at the Douglas Aircraft Company at Tucson, Arizona, for a training course. They would make history by being the first RAF crew to launch a Thor missile. *(Crown Copyright/Air Historical Branch image T-876)*

First RAF visit to Battersea helipad

The first RAF helicopter to land at the newly constructed helipad at Battersea, on the banks of the River Thames, did so on 29 April 1959. The aircraft was a Bristol Sycamore HR.14 (XG540) of the Central Flying School based at RAF South Cerney.

◄ The first RAF helicopter to land at the newly constructed helipad at Battersea, was XG540, a Bristol Sycamore HR.14 of the Central Flying School based at RAF South Cerney, 29 April 1959. *(Crown Copyright/Air Historical Branch image T-944)*

➤ **Another view of Bristol Sycamore HR.14, XG540, approaching to land on the recently constructed helipad at Battersea, alongside the River Thames.** *(Crown Copyright/Air Historical Branch image PRB-1-16577)*

◀ Two Vulcan B.1 aircraft based at RAF Waddington, XA912 and XH505 of 101 Squadron and 230 Operational Conversion Unit respectively, in formation on 11 May 1959. Both aircraft are fitted with the 'Phase 1' wing with a distinctive kink in the leading edge to improve the handling of the aircraft when manoeuvring at altitude. *(Crown Copyright/Air Historical Branch image PRB-1-16589)*

Farewell to the flying boat

In the Far East, all operational flying for the RAF's remaining Sunderland flying boats ceased on 15 May 1959. The Chief of the Air Staff sent a message to all commands of the RAF and to the Commonwealth Air Forces, part of which read: 'The cessation of operations by the two remaining Sunderlands of 205 Squadron on 15 May marks the end of another chapter in the history of the Royal Air Force. To all of us it is a sad occasion, as flying boats have been in continuous employment since the birth of the Royal Air Force in 1918, and in the Royal Navy service since before that.'

The last operational flight by an RAF flying boat, a Sunderland GR.5 – DP198/W – of No 205 Squadron, Seletar, Singapore, was made on 15 May. It was flown over Singapore Harbour by its 205 Squadron crew, led by the Squadron Commander, Wing Commander R.A.N. McCready OBE.

◀ The last Short Sunderland flying boat in RAF service, a Mark V, serial number DP198/W, making its final flight over Singapore Harbour on 15 May 1959 with Wing Commander R.A.N. McCready at the controls. *(Crown Copyright/ Air Historical Branch image CFP-985)*

RAF apprentices of No 1 School of Technical Training (1 SoTT) at RAF Halton are shown how to arm the Hawker Hunter's gun pack for Aden 20mm cannon. The apprentices are watching an instructor load a mock gun pack on to an instructional airframe, 14 April 1959. *(Crown Copyright/Air Historical Branch image T-1130)*

RAF technical apprentices under instruction at 1 SoTT RAF Halton, July 1959. The students are seated at desks in a workshop and a number of Hawker Hunter instructional airframes are located in the background, including F.1s 7510M (previously WT694/Y) and 7506M (previously WT595). *(Crown Copyright/Air Historical Branch image T-1136)*

UK–Cape Town record

On 9 July 1959, a Valiant of 214 Squadron, captained by Wing Commander M.J. Beetham, carried out the first non-stop flight from the UK to Cape Town (6,060 miles in 11 hours and 28 minutes) with the aid of air-to-air refuelling. Beetham, a former Second World War bomber pilot, went on to become Marshal of the Royal Air Force. As Chief of the Air Staff during the Falklands War he was involved in the decision to send the Task Force to the South Atlantic.

▼ In-service trials to develop in-flight refuelling techniques continued into 1959 and culminated in a record-breaking non-stop flight from the UK to Cape Town by a Valiant of 214 Squadron commanded by Wing Commander Michael Beetham, a future Chief of the Air Staff. This photograph was released in August 1959 and shows two aircraft of Marham-based 214 Squadron – Valiant BK.1, XD870, refuelling WZ390, a standard B.1 aircraft. *(Crown Copyright/Air Historical Branch image PRB-1-16962)*

Blériot Anniversary Air Race

One of the more light-hearted challenges of the year was the RAF's participation in the *Daily Mail* Blériot Anniversary Air Race from Marble Arch to the Arc de Triomphe. The race was held from 13–23 July 1959, to allow the maximum opportunity for the 135 participating teams to complete their journeys.

While the top prize of £5,000 was awarded to the team who completed the journey in the shortest time, a number of other prizes were on offer. This included a prize of £1,000 on the basis of the journey time, originality, ingenuity and initiative which went to the BEAline syndicate, a group of eleven men and two women from British European Airways who made the exceptionally good average time of 62 minutes and 15 seconds for their journey. It was made by special double-decker bus from Marble Arch to Paddington station, special diesel train to Ruislip Gardens, cars to Northolt, Comet 4B to Le Bourget and taxis to the Arc de Triomphe!

One object of the race was to focus attention on the need to speed up public transport journey times between the two city centres and the BEAline entry was especially significant in indicating what could be achieved.

Bill Aston, the Chief Production Test Pilot of Vickers-Armstrong, used a Piaggio P.136 amphibian for the race and was awarded a prize for 'initiative and practical demonstration of amphibian aircraft operations between the two cities'.

One of the unrewarded entries was that of Jean Salis, who flew his replica of Blériot's 1909 monoplane from Calais to Lydd. Another was Derek Piggott, who after making one trip each way in an EoN Primary glider towed by a Messenger, made a free-soaring flight over the Channel in an Olympia 419 glider in difficult conditions on 22 July. Several other entrants used the Air Charter and Silver City cross-Channel air ferries, in vehicles ranging from Lord Montagu's 1909 Humber to Freddie Laker's Rolls-Royce Silver Cloud and a Heinkel bubble car.

The RAF entered four teams into the race: Group Captain Ryder, the Station Commander at RAF Duxford; Squadron Leader C.G. Maughan, OC 56 Squadron at Duxford; Flight Lieutenant Williams, a pilot from the same squadron; and Under Officer Volkers, a cadet from RAF Cranwell. A few days before the race, the RAF race team assembled at RAF Duxford to make plans for their assault on the competition and it was planned with typical military precision!

After much detailed planning it was decided that competing pilots should travel on the pillion of RAF motorcycles from Marble Arch to the Thames Embankment near Chelsea Bridge, from there down a slippery pole onto a mud bank (which meant the state of the tide would dictate the time of the flight) where a helicopter would be waiting for a quick flight to RAF Biggin Hill. The RAF team had worked out that precious time and energy could be saved if a two-seat Hunter was used, so that the pilot could be taxiing for take-off while the competitor was strapping himself in and getting his breath back after the motorcycle and helicopter dash from the city centre. Competing officers were therefore supported by a team of Hunter pilots, co-ordinating officers, air traffic control officers and ground servicing staff, and their eventual narrow victory was the result of meticulous preparation and a very high level of teamwork.

From RAF Biggin Hill, the flight was by Hunter T.7 to Villacoublay, from whence the competitors flew by helicopter to Issy heliport on the left bank of the Seine, leaving a four-minute motorcycle dash to the Arc de Triomphe.

The journey in the opposite direction was done over the same route and eventually proved the faster direction. The eventual winner was Squadron Leader Maughan, who completed the journey in just 40 minutes and 44 seconds. Flight Lieutenant Williams achieved the second fastest time but was disqualified as his motorcycle driver failed to notice a red traffic light in London, when he went dashing past at around 80mph!

The prizes were presented at Marble Arch on 22 July by Lord Rothermere, Chairman of Associated Newspaper Group. The RAF's £5,000 first prize was divided by the Air Council between the RAF Benevolent Fund, The Soldiers', Sailors' and Airmen's Families Association and Paraplegics Sports Endowment Fund.

One of the RAF competitors taking part in the 1959 *Daily Mail* London–Paris Air Race, held to mark the 50th anniversary of Louis Blériot's crossing of the English Channel, dashes from a Sycamore HR.12 (WV791) to a waiting Hunter T.7. The race, which took place over several days in July 1959, could be attempted in either direction. It was won by Squadron Leader Charles Maughan, Officer Commanding 65 Squadron, who completed a run from the Arc de Triomphe to Marble Arch on 22 July in 40 minutes and 44 seconds, under a minute ahead of his nearest rival. Maughan used an RAF motorcycle for the first stage of his journey from the Arc de Triomphe to Issy, before climbing into a Sycamore of the Central Flying School for the flight to a waiting Hunter T.7 at Villacoublay. The aircraft landed at Biggin Hill 18½ minutes later, leaving the squadron leader to join another Sycamore for a short trip to Chelsea before a final motorcycle ride to Marble Arch. *(Crown Copyright/Air Historical Branch image PRB-1-17115)*

➤ A few days before the race, the RAF team assembled at RAF Duxford to meticulously plan the race. Their careful preparation and very high level of teamwork certainly paid off. *(Crown Copyright/Air Historical Branch image PRB-1-17114)*

An unidentified Hunter T.7 (coded 'T') of 56 Squadron being prepared for flight at RAF Biggin Hill during the *Daily Mail* Blériot Anniversary Air Race. In order to minimise lost time, the Hunter T.7 would have its engine running and ready to taxi when the competitor jumped into the aircraft for the relatively short flight from Duxford to Villacoublay. *(Crown Copyright/Air Historical Branch image PRB-1-17110)*

➤ With the preparatory pre-flight engineering work complete, Sycamore HR.12 WV781 prepares to start at RAF Biggin Hill, ready to receive its passenger for the short hop to the Thames Embankment at Chelsea Bridge. *(Crown Copyright/Air Historical Branch image PRB-1-17116)*

The RAF competitors utilised Sycamore HR.12 helicopters for the short legs between the Thames Embankment at Chelsea Bridge and Biggin Hill, and from Villacoublay to Issy heliport on the left bank of the Seine. Here, Sycamore HR.12 WV781 is prepared by the groundcrew while the pilot waits to start the engines at RAF Biggin Hill. *(Crown Copyright/Air Historical Branch image PRB-1-17113)*

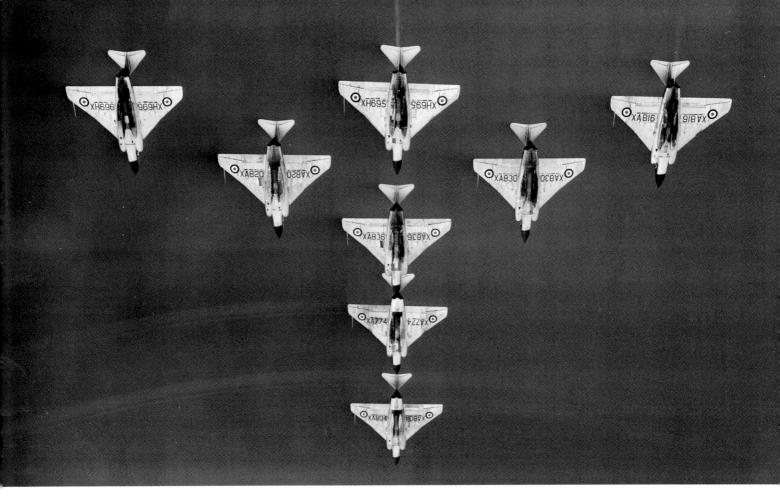

An interesting eight-ship formation view of 85 Squadron Javelin aircraft – both FAW.2s and FAW.6s – photographed on 13 June 1959. The only difference between the two marks was the increased fuel capacity of the later aircraft (an additional 230 gallons). For the record, the aircraft are: FAW.2s, XA774 and XA804; FAW.6s, XA816, 820, 830, 836, XH695 and 696. No 85 Squadron took delivery of the first Javelin FAW.2 aircraft in November 1958 and they remained with the squadron until March 1960. The FAW.6 aircraft were received into service at the same time but stayed with the squadron until June 1960. *(Above: Crown Copyright/Air Historical Branch image PRB-1-17183; below: Crown Copyright/Air Historical Branch image PRB-1-17185)*

In 1959, owing to their success and the demand for their appearance, 111 Squadron's display team, The Black Arrows, flew no fewer than fifty-five displays. For the Battle of Britain 'At Home' days in September alone, they appeared at Gaydon, Coltishall, Felixstowe and Wattisham. They are seen here in 'Big Nine' formation during a practice display. *(Crown Copyright/Air Historical Branch image T-1003)*

21 Squadron Scottish Aviation Twin Pioneer CC.1, XM958, seen during a flight from Benson, Oxfordshire, in June 1959, shortly after the squadron had officially reformed on 1 May 1959. *(Crown Copyright/Air Historical Branch image T-966)*

In April 1959, 21 Squadron at RAF Benson became the first UK-based squadron to receive the Twin Pioneer short take-off and landing transport. Four of the squadron's aircraft are pictured in formation on 13 August 1959. 21 Squadron took four of their Twin Pioneers to Khormaksar in June 1965 where they served successfully alongside 24 Infantry Brigade on internal security duties. The military version of the Twin Pioneer made its first flight on 29 August 1957. A total of thirty-nine Twin Pioneers were ordered by the RAF and the first joined 78 Squadron, then based in Aden. *(Crown Copyright/Air Historical Branch image PRB-1-17300)*

Three different aircraft types based at RAF Wyton performed a formation flypast over Ely Cathedral on 28 August 1959. Leading the flight is Victor B(PR).1, XA935 (nominally allocated to RAF Wyton), with Valiant B(PR)K.1, WZ391, of 543 Squadron, and an unknown Canberra PR.7 (thought to be WJ815) of 58 Squadron. For many years Wyton was the centre of RAF strategic reconnaissance, an association which ended with the disbandment of 543 Squadron (then flying Victor SR.2s) in May **1974**. *(Crown Copyright/Air Historical Branch image PRB-1-17304)*

Two generations of RAF fighters photographed in August 1959 during rehearsals for the Battle of Britain Flypast the following month. A Spitfire LF.XVI (TE476) and Hurricane IIc (LF363) of the Battle of Britain Flight are seen in formation with a Hawker Hunter F.6 (XF511/P) of 74 Squadron and a Gloster Javelin FAW.7 (XH958) of 23 Squadron. *(Crown Copyright/Air Historical Branch image T-1163)*

Four Handley Page Victor B.1s – XH588, 591, 592 and 589 – of 15 Squadron, RAF Cottesmore, photographed in flight in September 1959. All of these aircraft were later converted to B.1A standard, when ECM equipment was added. Along with 10 Squadron, No 15 Squadron formed part of the V-Force Wing at Cottesmore; the other wing being located at RAF Honington (with Nos 55 and 57 Squadrons). Victor B.1 aircraft arrived with 15 Squadron in September 1958 and remained with them until the squadron was disbanded in October 1964. *(Crown Copyright/Air Historical Branch image T-1186)*

President Dwight D. Eisenhower arriving at RAF Benson on 29 September 1959, after returning from a visit to Balmoral. The US President had flown in XK715, named *Columba*, a Comet C.2 of 216 Squadron, captained by Squadron Leader P.E. Pullan AFC. *(Left: Crown Copyright/Air Historical Branch image PRB-1-17640; below: Crown Copyright/Air Historical Branch image PRB-1-17641)*

⋀ Three Avro Vulcan B.1 aircraft photographed in formation during a sortie from RAF Waddington in September 1959. The aircraft are XH503 of 44 Squadron, along with XA896 and XH504 of 230 Operational Conversion Unit. *(Crown Copyright/Air Historical Branch image T-1211)*

Whispering Giant enters service

The introduction of the Britannia to RAF service in June 1959 provided Transport Command with its first turboprop transport aircraft. The Britannia operated widely on long-range strategic missions in many parts of the world, forming the basis for the rapid deployment of the army's United Kingdom Strategic Reserve Force.

The decision to order the military version of the Britannia, which had first flown as a civil airliner in August 1952, was taken in November 1955 when the projected Vickers V.1000 pure jet transport was cancelled. Six aircraft were initially ordered in January 1956; this was increased to ten and finally twenty-three. The first Britannia for the RAF (XL635) made its maiden flight at Belfast on 29 December 1958. The final Britannia was delivered on 2 January 1960.

Initial deliveries went to 99 Squadron and were followed by 511 Squadron, both units based at RAF Lyneham. Following defence cutbacks, the Britannia was retired from RAF service with the disbandment of 99 and 511 Squadrons in January 1976. They were all sold to civilian customers who continued to operate them around the world for many years.

SBAC Show highlights

The SBAC Show, held at Farnborough from 7–13 September, was a smaller affair than it had been in previous years, reflecting the continued contraction of the British aviation industry. The highlights were the first appearance of the Fairey Rotodyne (XE521) along with the first production Folland Gnat T.1 advanced jet trainer (XM691). The flying programme featured a sixteen-aircraft loop by the Hunter F.6s of 111 Squadron's Black Arrows and an interesting line of helicopters during the show including the Westland Westminster (G-APLE), Westland Wessex HAS.1 (XM301), Westland Whirlwind HAR.5 (XJ398), Westland Whirlwind 2 (G-AOCZ), Westland Widgeon (G-ANLW), Saunders-Roe P.531 (G-APVL) and Westland Skeeter (G-APOI), all taking to the air and hovering in front of the crowd line.

▼ **The highlight for many attending the 1959 SBAC Show at Farnborough was the formation display by sixteen Hawker Hunter F.6 fighters of The Black Arrows. The team, led by Squadron Leader Pete Latham, opened their display with a sixteen-aircraft loop and continued with the large formation during four manoeuvres. Seven then broke away in a downward bomb-burst, trailing smoke, while the nine-aircraft formation continued its routine. The show concluded with the nine performing a loop, followed by a downward bomb-burst while the remaining seven aircraft ran in before pulling up into a climb – offering some interesting head-on moments!** *(Crown Copyright/Air Historical Branch image PRB-1-17656)*

▲ Two versions of the Lightning prepare to start their flying display during the SBAC Show at Farnborough in September 1959. On the left is the ill-fated first prototype of the T.4 trainer, XL628, with XG331, one of a batch of twenty pre-production P.1B aircraft produced to assist the flight development of the F23/49 project, and commonly referred to as the Development Batch. XL628 crashed during a test flight on 1 October 1959 when the fin collapsed during a turn and the pilot abandoned the aircraft over the Irish Sea. Squadron service for the Lightning was still some nine months away, with 74 Squadron at Coltishall not receiving the first Lightning F.1s until June 1960. *(Crown Copyright/Air Historical Branch image PRB-1-17663)*

▼ An early pre-production Bristol Belvedere HC.1, XG451, lifting a dummy Bloodhound surface-to-air missile during a display at the SBAC Show at Farnborough in September 1959. The first operational unit of the RAF to be equipped with the Belvedere was 66 Squadron at RAF Odiham, which took delivery in September 1961. The Belvedere had a relatively short military career and was retired from RAF service in March 1969. *(Crown Copyright/Air Historical Branch image T-1215)*

The prototype Fairey Rotodyne, XE521, displaying at the SBAC Show at Farnborough in September 1959. The prototype Rotodyne had made its first flight at White Waltham on 6 November 1957, but the project was cancelled in February 1962 and no further examples were constructed. While the helicopter is no longer complete, some sections of it are preserved at the Helicopter Museum at Weston-super-Mare. *(Crown Copyright/Air Historical Branch image T-1222)*

A line-up of various British-built helicopters at the SBAC Show at Farnborough in September 1959, with the Westland Westminster (G-APLE) nearest the camera. *(Crown Copyright/Air Historical Branch image T-1216)*

◄ At the end of 1958, 78 Squadron at Khormaksar became the first squadron to operate the Scottish Aviation Twin Pioneer CC.1 light transport aircraft. The aircraft, like its predecessor, the single Pioneer, possessed excellent short-field capabilities which proved useful when flying supplies in to remote, unprepared landing strips around the Gulf and Far East regions where many of the thirty-nine examples were based. This picture, taken in September 1959, shows Twin Pioneer CC.1, XM286, one of the first aircraft to join 78 Squadron, flying over Aden, with the port below. *(Crown Copyright/Air Historical Branch image CMP-1090)*

⋁ Wing Commander N. Poole, Commanding Officer of 33 Squadron, in his personally marked Javelin FAW.7, XH835/NP, during a training sortie from RAF Middleton St George in September 1959. *(Crown Copyright/Air Historical Branch image PRB-1-17786)*

➤ Parachutists of the RAF Parachute Brigade photographed boarding Blackburn Beverley C.1, XB268/D, of 53 Squadron, via the rear loading steps into the aircraft's capacious tail boom during Exercise Red Banner, 12 October 1959. The week-long joint army/RAF exercise was designed to test the deployment of rapid reaction airborne forces and their subsequent support by helicopter while in the field. *(Crown Copyright/Air Historical Branch image T-1283)*

Gloster Javelin FAW.7, XH756/A, of 23 Squadron based at RAF Coltishall, carrying four Firestreak infra-red air-to-air homing missiles during a sortie on 12 November 1959. *(Above: Crown Copyright/Air Historical Branch image T-849; right: Crown Copyright/Air Historical Branch image T-851)*

Whirlwind joins the Queen's Flight

On 5 November 1959, two Westland Whirlwind HCC.8 helicopters (XN126 and XN127) were handed over to the Queen's Flight at the manufacturer's factory in Yeovil. After service with the Queen's Flight at RAF Benson, they were later converted to HAR.10 standards and used in normal RAF squadron use.

▼ The two Westland Whirlwind HCC.8 helicopters used by the Queen's Flight, XN126 and XN127, pictured shortly after being handed over at the manufacturer's factory at Yeovil on 5 November 1959. The two helicopters were immediately flown to join the unit at RAF Benson. Powered by 740hp Leonides Major 160 engines, they were the only helicopters in the RAF equipped with these engines. Both helicopters were fitted with dual controls and had special soundproofing and furnishings in the four-seat cabin. Both were later converted to HAR.10 standard. *(Crown Copyright/Air Historical Branch image T-1702)*

A decade of change

The 1950s opened with the Royal Air Force operating Avro Lincoln long-range heavy bombers and Mosquito, Hornet and Spitfire fighter aircraft, along with other obsolete propeller-driven types. It had a transport fleet that was benefiting from the recent delivery of Handley Page Hastings aircraft, a training fleet operating Prentice, Athena and Anson aircraft – and the Chipmunk was about to enter service. Much of the equipment in use were relics remaining from the Second World War. There were *some* jet aircraft in the inventory – Meteors and Venoms among them – while helicopters were very much a thing of potential.

By way of a striking contrast, the decade finished with Bomber Command operating a nuclear-equipped V-bomber force of Valiant, Vulcan and Victor, ably supported by the English Electric Canberra. In-flight air-to-air refuelling had been perfected by the Valiant force. Transport Command operated the Comet 2C and Bristol Britannia, supported by the load-carrying Beverley. Training Command had all-jet through training with the Jet Provost. Fighter Command had a fleet of all-weather Hawker Hunter and Javelin aircraft. The English Electric P.1B, a Mach 2 interceptor, would soon be arriving.

For the Royal Air Force, the 1950s was clearly a decade of spectacular change.

Aircraft on strength, by year

RAF aircraft and establishment on strength as at 31 December of:

	1950(1) Auth'd	1950(1) Strength	1951 Auth'd	1951 Strength	1952 Auth'd	1952 Strength	1953 Auth'd	1953 Strength
HOME COMMANDS								
Bomber	331	327	374	345	391	407	474	455
Coastal	120	114	168	148	204	193	200	218
Fighter (Regular)	831	872	888	88	1051	1047	1122	1031
Fighter (RAuxAF)	300	328	300	336	281	275	241	246
Transport	166	186	158	190	190	194	176	200
Home (2)	978	760	986	981	1302	1049	572	575
Flying Training	978	943	1437	1391	1785	1798	1376	1361
Technical Training	58	55	53	52	49	54	41	55
Maintenance	57	63	58	59	18	27	15	24
90 Signals Group	50	49	62	61	72	68	57	59
TOTAL	3869	3697	4484	3651	5343	5112	4274	4224
OVERSEAS								
Germany	252	262	327	327	532	489	679	711
MEAF/Gulf/Malta	282	343	316	488	315	402	314	378
Far East	212	319	225	313	267	327	285	372
Rhodesia	116	225	142	278	142	211		
TOTAL	862	1149	1010	1406	1256	1429	1278	1461
OTHER								
Special Duties List	26	27	24	27	17	20	15	17
GRAND TOTAL	4757	4873	5518	5084	6616	6561	5567	5702

	Estab	Strength	Estab	Strength	Estab	Strength	Estab	Strength
MANPOWER (3)								
Other Ranks – Regular (4)	No information available		170356	121817	188747	133198	196904	143007
Other Ranks – National Service				64845		58161		50980
Other Ranks – Aircrew (5)				4938		4963		4700
Officers – GD (Air) Branch (6)				10312		14137		13305
Officers – Other Branches (7)				13722		14268		14784
TOTAL				215634		224727		226776

Notes:
(1) January 1951 figures
(2) Absorbed in Flying Training Command 1 April 1959
(3) Trained strength
(4) Strength includes: airmen and WRAF
(5) Ranks: Master Aircrew, Flight Sergeant, Sergeant – December 1950–59; Master Aircrew, Pilot I, Pilot II, Pilot III, Pilot IV – January 1950–October 1951
(6) GD = General Duties (Air) Branches: Pilot, Navigator, Signaller, Engineer, Gunner, Bomber and Electronics
(7) Includes Princess Mary's Royal Air Force Nursing Service and WRAF

| 1954 | | 1955 | | 1956 | | 1957 | | 1958 | | 1959 | |
Auth'd	Strength	Auth'd	Strength	Auth'd	Strength	Auth'd	Strength	Auth'd	Strength	Auth'd	Strength
485	478	468	481	452	456	414	403	397	398	328	334
215	214	228	220	181	170	139	140	135	140	121	130
1202	1183	1363	1269	1247	1270	913	962	678	705	595	603
241	209	242	223	242	260						
179	180	171	168	191	202	156	161	158	170	164	166
406	384	403	410	377	375	225	226	169	185	687	716
42	49	808	759	767	776	704	726	634	666		
843	932	41	46	40	40	38	42	45	45	45	46
38	40	14	16	13	13	14	15	16	17	19	25
13	22	43	47	44	48	43	50	43	43	44	45
3664	3691	3781	3639	3554	3610	2646	2725	2275	2369	2003	2065

| 1954 | | 1955 | | 1956 | | 1957 | | 1958 | | 1959 | |
Auth'd	Strength	Auth'd	Strength	Auth'd	Strength	Auth'd	Strength	Auth'd	Strength	Auth'd	Strength
721	711	667	682	635	635	332	330	306	300	303	311
282	369	247	349	259	336	181	243	197	249	194	234
302	373	256	301	237	301	153	204	147	200	110	141
1305	1453	1170	1332	1131	1272	666	777	650	749	607	686

| 1954 | | 1955 | | 1956 | | 1957 | | 1958 | | 1959 | |
Auth'd	Strength	Auth'd	Strength	Auth'd	Strength	Auth'd	Strength	Auth'd	Strength	Auth'd	Strength
13	14	17	15	15	14	9	10	9	9	9	8
4982	5158	4968	4986	4700	4896	3321	3512	2934	3127	2619	2759

Estab	Strength	Estab	Strength	Estab	Strength	Estab	Strength	Estab	Strength	Estab	Strength
185418	140354	184638	126706	177388	115975	152460	108309	133360	102929	124840	105715
	46520		48174		56857		43988		23436		14365
	4169		3981		3831		3350		3378		2965
	12565		12190		11920		11595		10566		10394
	14419		14249		14258		13852		12615		12204
	218027		205300		202841		181094		152924		145643

Sources:
RAF Form Stats 603 – Monthly Statement of Aircraft Authorised and on Hand in the RAF
RAF Form Stats 1204 – Monthly Record Office Return Establishment and Mustered Strength of Ground Personnel by Trades
RAF Form Stats 216 – Monthly Record Office Return of Officers by Branch and Rank and at Quarter Months by Type of Commission
RAF Form Stats 217 – Monthly Record Office Return of Regular Airmen (Aircrew) by Category and Rank

Queen's Review flypast aircraft

Formation number	Time over Odiham	Aircraft type and quantity	Command	Base	Speed (mph)	Height (ft)
1	3:39½	1 × Sycamore	Fighter	Blackbushe	86	400
2	3:40	16 × Chipmunk	Home	Booker	98	600
3	3:40½	16 × Chipmunk	Flying Training	South Cerney	98	800
4	3:41	12 × Prentice	Flying Training	South Cerney	98	600
5	3:41½	12 × Harvard	Flying Training	Little Rissington	138	800
6	3:42	12 × Oxford	Flying Training	Wellesbourne-Mountford	138	600
7	3:42½	12 × Anson	Flying Training	Shawbury	138	800
8	3:43	12 × Balliol	Flying Training	Cottesmore	166	600
9	3:43½	6 × Varsity	Flying Training	Thorney Island	166	1,100
10	3:44	6 × Varsity	Flying Training	Thorney Island	166	600
11	3:44½	6 × Valetta	Transport/Maintenance	Colerne	166	1,100
12	3:45	3 × Sunderland	Coastal	Pembroke Dock	150	1,200
13	3:45½	9 × Lincoln	Bomber	Upwood	166	700
14	3:46½	9 × Lincoln	Bomber	Upwood	166	1,200
15	3:47½	9 × Lincoln	Bomber	Waddington	166	700
16	3:48	9 × Lincoln	Bomber	Waddington	166	1,200
17	3:48½	9 × Lincoln	Bomber	Hemswell	166	700
18	3:49½	12 × Washington	Bomber	Marham	195	1,200
19	3:50½	9 × Shackleton	Coastal	St Eval	195	700
20	3:51	9 × Shackleton	Coastal	Ballykelly/Aldergrove	195	1,200
21	3:51½	5 × Neptune	Coastal	Kinloss	195	700
22	3:52½	3 × Hastings	Transport/Maintenance	Lyneham	195	1,200
23	3:53½	12 × Vampire NF.10	Fighter	Coltishall	305	700
24	3:54	12 × Vampire FB.5	RAAF	Horsham St Faith	305	1,200
25	3:54½	12 × Vampire FB.5	Flying Training	Oakington	305	700
26	3:55	12 × Meteor F.4	Flying Training	Oakington	345	1,200
27	3:55½	24 × Venom FB.1	2 TAF	Wattisham	345	700
28	3:56	24 × Meteor F.8	Fighter	Tangmere	345	1,200
29	3:56½	24 × Meteor F.8	Fighter	Biggin Hill	345	700
30	3:57	24 × Meteor F.8	Fighter	Duxford	345	1,200
31	3:57½	24 × Meteor F.8	Fighter	Horsham St Faith	345	700
32	3:58	24 × Meteor F.8	Fighter	Waterbeach	345	1,200

Formation number	Time over Odiham	Aircraft type and quantity	Command	Base	Speed (mph)	Height (ft)
33	3:58½	24 × Meteor F.8	Fighter	Honiley	345	700
34	3:59	24 × Meteor F.8	Fighter	Wattisham	345	1,200
35	3:59½	24 × Meteor F.8	Fighter	Wymeswold	345	700
36	4:00	24 × Meteor F.8	Fighter	North Weald	345	1,200
37	4:00½	18 × Meteor NF.11	Fighter	West Malling	345	700
38	4:01	18 × Meteor NF.11	Fighter	West Malling	345	1,200
39	4:01½	24 × Canberra	Bomber	Binbrook	345	700
40	4:02	24 × Canberra	Bomber	Hemswell/ Scampton	345	1,200
41	4:02½	24 × Sabre	2 TAF	Duxford	345	700
42	4:03	36 × Sabre	RCAF	North Luffenham	345	1,200
43	4:03½	6 × Swift F.1	Fighter	Boscombe Down	460	700
44	4:04½	1 × Victor	Ministry of Supply	Radlett	288	1,200
45	4:05	1 × Valiant	Ministry of Supply	Wisley	345	1,200
46	4:05½	1 × Vulcan	Ministry of Supply	Woodford	460	1,200
47	4:06	1 × Javelin	Ministry of Supply	Moreton Valence	575	700
48	4:06½	1 × Hunter	Ministry of Supply	Dunsford	667	700
49	4:07	1 × Swift F.4	Ministry of Supply	Chilbolton	667	700

⋁ Hawker Hunter FGA.9 aircraft of 8 Squadron, led by their Commanding Officer, Squadron Leader R. Knight, seen during a formation flypast over Aden Protectorate from their base at Khormaksar in 1959. *(Crown Copyright/Air Historical Branch image CMP-1113)*

Bibliography

Barnes, C.H., *Bristol Aircraft Since 1910,* 1st edition, Putnam & Company, 1964.

British Aviation Research Group, *British Military Aircraft Serials and Markings*, 2nd edition, BARG/Nostalgair/The Aviation Hobby Shop, 1983.

By Command of the Defence Council, *The Malayan Emergency 1948–1960*, Ministry of Defence, 1970.

Wing Commander J.R. Dowling MBE DFC* AFC CFS* AMRAes RAF (Retd), *RAF Helicopters – The First Twenty Years (Part 1)*, Air Historical Branch, 1987.

Wing Commander J.R. Dowling MBE DFC* AFC CFS* AMRAes RAF (Retd), *RAF Helicopters – The First Twenty Years (Part 2)*, Air Historical Branch, 1987.

Ellis, Ken, *Wrecks & Relics*, 21st edition, Crecy Publishing, 2008.

Flintham, Victor, *Air Wars and Aircraft – A Detailed Record of Air Combat, 1945 to the Present,* Arms and Armour Press, 1989.

Flintham, Victor and Andrew Thomas, *Combat Codes – A Full Explanation And Listing of British, Commonwealth and Allied Air Force Unit Codes Since 1938*, Pen & Sword Aviation, 2008.

Jackson, Robert, *V-Force: Britain's Airborne Nuclear Deterrent*, Ian Allan Publishing, 2000.

James, Derek N., *Westland Aircraft Since 1915*, Putnam, 1995.

Air Chief Marshal Sir David Lee GBE CB, *Flight from the Middle East*, Air Historical Branch, 1978.

Air Chief Marshal Sir David Lee GBE CB, *Wings in the Sun – A History of the Royal Air Force in the Mediterranean, 1945–1986*, HMSO, 1989.

Martin, Bernard, *The Viking, Valetta and Varsity*, Air Britain Publications, 1975.

Air Commodore Graham Pitchfork, *The Royal Air Force Day by Day*, Sutton Publishing, 2008.

Ritchie, Dr Sebastian, *The RAF, Small Wars and Insurgencies in the Middle East, 1919–1939*, Air Historical Branch, 2011.

Ritchie, Dr Sebastian, *The RAF, Small Wars and Insurgencies: Later Colonial Operations, 1945–1975*, Air Historical Branch, 2011.

Robertson, Bruce, *British Military Aircraft Serials 1878–1987*, Midland Counties Publications, 1987.

Thetford, Owen, *Aircraft of the Royal Air Force Since 1918*, Putnam, 8th edition, 1988.

Trevenen James, A.G., *The Royal Air Force – the Past 30 Years*, McDonald and Jane's Publishers Limited, 1976.

Watkins, David, *The History of RAF Aerobatic Teams Since 1920*, Pen & Sword Aviation, 2010.

Index

1954

(Crown Copyright/Air Historical Branch Image Pub-INF217-FlyWithTheRAF)

1951

(Crown Copyright/Air Historical Branch Image Pub-INF168-RAF 40years)

1952

(Crown Copyright/Air Historical Branch Image Pub-INF132-GiveYourAmbitionWings)

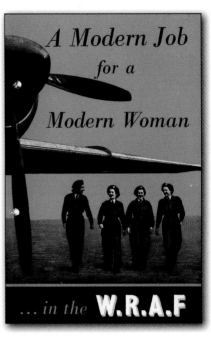

1952

(Crown Copyright/Air Historical Branch Image Pub-INF181-ModernJobForAModernWoman)

1953

(Crown Copyright/Air Historical Branch Image Pub-INF190-TheRAFRegiment)

1955

(Crown Copyright/Air Historical Branch Image Pub-INF194-SpareTimeServiceFC)

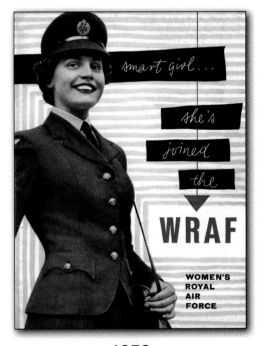

1956

(Crown Copyright/Air Historical Branch Image Pub-INF233-SmartGirl)

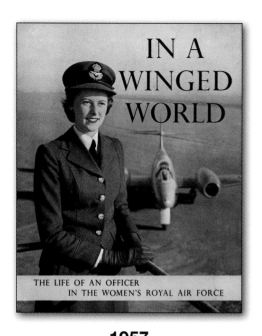

1957

(Crown Copyright/Air Historical Branch Image Pub-INF221-InAWingedWorld)

1958

(Crown Copyright/Air Historical Branch Image Pub-INF249-YourSonAndTheRAF)

1959

(Crown Copyright/Air Historical Branch Image Pub-INF276-LivingAtHomeintheWRAF)

1958

(Crown Copyright/Air Historical Branch Image Pub-INF267-RAF 40years)